$15.95

"If you are not experiencing the life you want, there is one person to whom you can turn to change your life, and that person is you.

You can begin to improve your life at any moment. It is largely your decision. If you are to experience satisfaction, it is more likely to happen if you formulate the thoughts that spur actions that create the situation more satisfying to you. Know that it is within your power and ability to do so."

– John McCabe, from his book *Igniting Your Life*

Books by John McCabe

Igniting Your Life:
Pathways to the Zenith of Health and Success

Voices of Reason
Quotations of Uplifting and Motivational
Philosophy from throughout History

Voices of Wisdom
Quotations of Uplifting and Motivational
Philosophy from throughout History

Voices of Insight
Quotations of Uplifting and Motivational
Philosophy from throughout History

Arise
Recovering, Revealing, and Ascending
into the Law of Manifestation

Sunfood Diet Infusion:
Transforming Health and Preventing
Disease through Raw Veganism

Raw Vegan Easy Healthy Recipes:
Simple, Low-fat, Health Infusing Cuisine

Vegan Truth Vegan Myth:
Obliterating Rumors and Lies about the Earth-Saving Diet that can
Save Your Life

Extinction:
The Death of Waterlife on Planet Earth

VOICES OF INSIGHT

Quotations of Uplifting & Motivational Philosophy from throughout History

John McCabe

Author of *Igniting Your Life*

Voices of Insight

Disclaimer:
This book is sold for information purposes only. How you interpret and utilize the information in this book is your decision. Neither the author nor the publisher and/or distributor will be held accountable for the use or misuse of the information contained in this book. This book is not intended as medical advice because the author and publisher of this work are not recommending the use of chemical drugs or surgery to alleviate health challenges. It also does not stand as legal advice, or suggest that you break any laws. Because of the way people interpret what they read, and take actions based on their own intellect and life situations, which are not in the author's, publisher's, and/or distributor's control, there is always some risk involved; therefore, the author, publisher, and/or distributor of this book are not responsible for any adverse effects or consequences from the use of any suggestions, foods, substances, products, procedures, or lifestyles described hereafter.

ISBN: 978-1-884702-20-4
First Edition: 2015

Copyright © 2014 by John McCabe
All intellectual rights owned by John McCabe and reserved in perpetuity throughout the universe. No part of the author's words in this book may be reproduced in any form or by any electronic, mechanical, or other means, including on the Internet, through cell phone and/or personal, educational, public, and/or business communication and technology systems, or through any and all information storage and retrieval systems, including book sample and publicity Web sites, without permission in writing from the author, and only the author, except by a reviewer, who may quote brief, attributed passages of the final published book in a review; and as fair use by authors wishing to use short, credited quotations of the author's words.

Introduction

In this, my third compilation of quotations I've collected throughout my life, I hope to continue inspiring people, influencing people, triggering their good side, and helping them focus on building satisfactory lives that are rewarding, satisfying, and part of the solution to what is ailing the planet.

Clearly, it is through thought that our actions and words are guided. If we engage in thinking thoughts that are more productive in sustainable ways, and are more in tune with what the world needs, what society needs, what the culture needs, what wildlife needs, and what we need, our lives will be part of the solution.

I am a person who has also struggled to figure and factor ways of being part of the solution. Living in a society that is so absorbed in greed, commercialism, and the raping of Earth for resources, it is easy to get lost, to lose focus, to become a wanderer, and to become part of the problems.

It seems that the human mind is in continual need of being guided onto pathways that are part of the solution, and to be guided off those that can become absorbable, misleading, discouraging, and saturated with all that we do not need in and out of life.

It is quotations like those in the following pages that have helped remind me of what it is I want of life. There were times where I was completely at a loss of what to do with myself. I didn't feel like I fit in. I didn't feel like I had a role model. I didn't see inspiration in the people around me. I felt disconnected from what I saw going on around me. And I felt driven to make my way onto a better path that could bring me to experience satisfaction and to feel as if I was making a difference for the better on the planet.

I have found satisfaction in writing the types of books I have written. And that alone is pretty amazing to me. I was one who didn't know how to read very well until I was a teenager. Teachers didn't seem to know what to do with me. They seemed to find me a curiosity. I wasn't one who blended in. I didn't tune into their training of spewing information and being tested on it. They saw that I had natural abilities that didn't seem to be part of standardized schooling methods.

We can all figure our ways. We can factor our solutions. We can use our talents and intellect, skills, graces, and other attributes to make things work for us. And hopefully in ways that benefit society, culture, wildlife, and Earth.

Dear reader, I hope this book is interesting to you, that it helps you factor your way onto paths that bring you satisfaction and bring you to be part of the solution of what the Earth needs, of what wildlife needs, and of what you need.

"Think and then think what you have thought. Is it really what you had thought. Think again."
– Amit Abraham

"Stories serve the purpose of consolidating whatever gains people or their leaders have made or imagine they have made in their existing journey through the world."
– Chinua Achebe

"Seeing ourselves as others see us would probably confirm our worst suspicions about them."
– Franklin P. Adams

"A teacher affects eternity; he can never tell where his influence stops."
– Henry Brooks Adams

"Abundance comes not from stuff. In fact, stuff is an indication of non-abundance. Abundance is in the sacred; it's in the connection of love. We will find abundance through hard times when we find each other."
– Rebecca Adamson

"The unique personality which is the real life in me, I can not gain unless I search for the real life, the spiritual quality, in others. I am myself spiritually dead unless I reach out to the fine quality dormant in others. For it is only with the god enthroned in the innermost shrine of the other, that the god hidden in me, will consent to appear."
– Felix Adler

"Reality is like a bud that keeps opening. The petals keep revealing themselves. It's not as if that bud becomes something that it wasn't before. It just keeps showing its potential."
– Adyashanti

"The truth is that you already are what you are seeking."
– Adyashanti

"Happiness is a choice that requires effort at times."
– Aeschylus

"Men often bear little grievances with less courage than they do large misfortunes."
– Aesop

"Better be wise by the misfortunes of others than by your own."
– Aesop

"Caring means doing."
– Andre Agassi

"By sowing frugality we reap liberty, a golden harvest."
– Agesilaus

"There's no limit to what you can dream. You *expect* the unexpected, you *believe* in magic, in fairy tales, and in possibilities. Then you grow older and that innocence is shattered and somewhere along the way the reality of *life* gets in the way and you're hit by the realization that you can't be *all* you wanted to be, you just might have to settle for a little bit less."
– Cecelia Ahern

"The heart is sometimes tainted with the songs of yesterday. Sing a new song today."
– Steven Aitchison

"Fear of what may happen in the future, and thinking about what happened in the past, shouldn't stop you doing something in the present."
– Steven Aitchison

"Dreams digest the meals that are our days."
– Astrid Alauda

"Each of us has a spark of life inside us, and our highest aspiration ought to be to set off that spark in one another."
– Mark Albion

"The simple act of caring is heroic."
– Edward Albert

"All parents damage their children. It cannot be helped. Youth, like pristine glass, absorbs the prints of its handlers. Some parents smudge, others crack, a few shatter childhoods completely into jagged little pieces, beyond repair."
– Mitch Alborn

"So many people walk around with a meaningless life. They seem half-asleep, even when they're busy doing things they think are important. This is because they're chasing the wrong things. The way you get meaning into your life is to devote yourself to loving others, devote yourself to your community around you, and devote yourself to creating something that gives you purpose and meaning."
– Mitch Alborn

"Love is the only thing that we can carry with us when we go, and it makes the end so easy."
– Louisa May Alcott

"The power of finding beauty in the humblest things makes home happy and life lovely."
– Louisa May Alcott

"I'm not afraid of storms, for I'm learning to sail my ship."
– Louisa May Alcott

"Have regular hours for work and play; make each day both useful and pleasant, and prove that you understand the worth of time by employing it well. Then youth will bring few regrets, and life will become a beautiful success."
– Louisa May Alcott

"Often romantic relationships fail because you are trying to get someone to fall in love with the YOU that you never discovered."
– Shannon L. Alder

"Fantasy is hardly an escape from reality. It's a way of understanding it."
– Lloyd Alexander

"The best way to make your dreams come true is to wake up."
– Muhammad Ali

"Beauty awakens the soul to act."
– Dante Alighieri

"Remember tonight... for it is the beginning of always"
– Dante Alighieri

"Dream lofty dreams, and as you dream, so shall you become. Your vision is the promise of what you shall one day be; your ideal is the prophecy of what you shall at last unveil."
– James Allen

"Life brings simple pleasures to us every day. It is up to us to make them wonderful memories."
– Cathy Allen

"Champions aren't made in the gyms. Champions are made from something they have deep inside them — a desire, a dream, a vision."
– Muhammad Ali

"The only competition worthy of a wise man is with himself."
– Washington Allston

"When you speak of someone or about someone, you should speak as though they were in the room with you. The ears that you speak to today are attached to the mouth that could relay the message tomorrow."
– William Biddy Allen

"Life is short and we have never too much time for gladdening the hearts of those who are traveling the dark journey with us. Oh be swift to love, make haste to be kind."
– Henri-Frederic Amiel

"Happiness is a continuous creative activity."
– Baba Amte

"When we are motivated by goals that have deep meaning, by dreams that need completion, by pure love that needs expressing — then we truly live life."
– Greg Anderson

"As long as you keep a person down, some part of you has to be down there to hold him down, so it means you cannot soar as you otherwise might."
– Marion Anderson

"I realized then that even though I was a tiny speck in an infinite cosmos, a blip on the timeline of eternity, I was not without purpose."
– R. J. Anderson

"Bad things do happen; how I respond to them defines my character and the quality of my life. I can choose to sit in perpetual sadness, immobilized by the

gravity of my loss, or I can choose to rise from the pain and treasure the most precious gift I have — life itself."
– Walter Anderson

"We're never so vulnerable as when we trust someone — but paradoxically, if we cannot trust, neither can we find love or joy."
– Walter Anderson

"I believe that the way people live can be directed a little by architecture."
– Tadao Ando

"Well, that's why smart people get tripped up with worry and fear. Worry…fear…is just a misuse of the creative imagination that has been placed in each of us. Because we are smart and creative, we imagine all the things that could happen, that might happen, that will happen if this or that happens. See what I mean?"
– Andy Andrews

"Some people regard discipline as a chore. For me, it is a kind of order that sets me free to fly."
– Julie Andrews

"Sometimes opportunities float right past your nose. Work hard, apply yourself, and be ready. When an opportunity comes you can grab it."
– Julie Andrews

"Circumstances may cause interruptions and delays, but never lose sight of your goal. Prepare yourself in every way you can by increasing your knowledge and adding to your experience, so that you can make the most of opportunity when it occurs."
– Mario Andretti

"Listen to yourself and in that quietude you might hear the voice of God."
– Maya Angelou

"Stepping onto a brand-new path is difficult, but not more difficult than remaining in a situation, which is not nurturing to the whole woman."
– Maya Angelou

"Each of us has the right and the responsibility to assess the roads which lie ahead, and those over which we have traveled, and if the future road looms ominous or unpromising, and the roads back uninviting, then we need to gather our resolve and, carrying only the necessary baggage, step off that road into another direction. If the new choice is also unpalatable, without embarrassment, we must be ready to change that as well."
– Maya Angelou

"When I look back, I am so impressed again with the life-giving power of literature. If I were a young person today, trying to gain a sense of myself in the world, I would do that again by reading, just as I did when I was young."
– Maya Angelou

"I've learned that people will forget what you said, people will forget what you did, but people will never forget how you made them feel."
– Maya Angelou

"When you complain, all you do is broadcast, 'There's a victim in the neighborhood.'"
– Maya Angelou

"When I look back, I am so impressed again with the life-giving power of literature. If I were a young person today, trying to gain a sense of myself in the world, I would do that again by reading, just as I did when I was young."
– Maya Angelou

"If you are always trying to be normal, you will never know how amazing you can be."
– Maya Angelou

"Make every effort to change things you do not like. If you cannot make a change, change the way you have been thinking. You might find a new solution."
– Maya Angelou

"I have never been a millionaire. But I have enjoyed a crackling fire, a glorious sunset, a walk with a friend, and a hug from a child. There are plenty of life's tiny delights for all of us."
– Jack Anthony

"Do not reveal your thoughts to everyone, lest you drive away your good luck."
– Apocrypha, Ecclesiasticus 8:19

"Nothing's perfect, the world's not perfect. But it's there for us, trying the best it can; that's what makes it so damn beautiful."
– Hiromu Arakawa

"Stand up and walk. Move on. After all, you have perfect legs to stand on."
– Hiromu Arakawa

"Pleasure in the job puts perfection in the work."
– Aristotle

"For the things we have to learn before we can do them, we learn by doing them."
– Aristotle

"Happiness is the meaning and the purpose of life, the whole aim and end of human existence."
– Aristotle

"We are what we repeatedly do. Excellence then is not an act, but a habit."
– Aristotle

"For the things we have to learn before we can do them, we learn by doing them."
– Aristotle

"Hope is a waking dream."
– Aristotle

"Stop looking outside yourself for your substantiation. Learn to love who you are."
– Alan Arkin

"Our passion is our strength."
– Billie Joe Armstrong

"I want you to have big dreams, big goals. I want you to strive to achieve them. But I don't want to see you beating yourself up every time you make a mistake."
– Kelley Armstrong

"If there is one thing I say to those who use me as their example, it's that if you ever get a second chance in life, you've got to go all the way."
– Lance Armstrong

"The freethinking of one age is the common sense of the next."
– Matthew Arnold

"I have found that if you love life, life will love you back."
– Lalit Arora

"Friendship is the marriage of the soul."
– François-Marie "Voltaire" Arouet

"The most important decision you make is to be in a good mood."
– François-Marie "Voltaire" Arouet

"Life is a shipwreck, but we must not forget to sing in the lifeboats."
– François-Marie "Voltaire" Arouet

"Shun idleness. It is a rust that attaches itself to the most brilliant of metals."
– François-Marie "Voltaire" Arouet

"Through our soul is our contact with heaven."
– Sholem Asch

"Never let your sense of morals prevent you from doing what is right."
– Isaac Asimov

"Self-education is, I firmly believe, the only kind of education there is."
– Isaac Asimov

"If journalism is good, it is controversial by its nature."
– Julian Assange

"Sanctify yourself and you will sanctify society."
– Saint Francis of Assisi

"This above all, to refuse to be a victim. Unless I can do that I can do nothing."
– Margaret Atwood

"Music washes away from the soul the dust of everyday life."
– Berthold Auerbach

"How much time he gains who does not look to see what his neighbor says or does or thinks, but only at what he does himself, to make it just and holy."
– Marcus Aurelius

"Accept whatever comes to you woven in the pattern of your destiny, for what could more aptly fit your needs?"
– Marcus Aurelius

"Don't go on discussing what a good person should be. Just be one."
– Marcus Aurelius

"Remember this, that very little is needed to make a happy life."
– Marcus Aurelius

"The happiness of your life depends on the quality of your thoughts."
– Marcus Aurelius

"When you arise in the morning, think of what a privilege it is to be alive: to breathe, to think, to enjoy, to love."
– Marcus Aurelius

"A man's life is what his thoughts make it."
— Marcus Aurelius

"Our life is what our thoughts make it."
— Marcus Aurelius

"When you arise in the morning think of what a privilege it is to be alive, to think, to enjoy, to love."
— Marcus Aurelius

"It is not death that a man should fear, but he should fear never beginning to live."
— Marcus Aurelius

"Do not give way to useless alarm; though it is right to be prepared for the worst, there is no occasion to look on it as certain."
— Jane Austen

"Vision is the foresight or forecast or insight into the future. Vision is the picture of one's destiny or accomplishment, or simply what a person is meant to do or become."
— Israelmore Avivor

"Science is a wondrously successful way of knowing the world, but it isn't the only way. Knowledge also derives from other sources, such as common-sense experience, imaginative literature, music, and artistic expression."
— Francisco Ayala

B

"Before you speak, ask yourself: Is it kind? It is necessary? Is it true? Does it improve on the silence?"
– Shirdi Sai Baba

"If you want to meet someone who can fix any situation you don't like, who can bring you happiness in spite of what other people say or believe, look in a mirror and say this magic word: Hello."
– Richard Bach

"No matter how qualified or deserving you are, you will never reach a better life until you can imagine it for yourself and allow yourself to have it."
– Richard Bach

"The worst men often give the best advice."
– Francis Bacon

"Begin doing what you want to do now. We are not living in eternity. We have only this moment, sparkling like a star in our hand--and melting like a snowflake."
– Francis Bacon

"A man who studieth revenge keeps his own wounds green."
– Francis Bacon

"In today's environment, hoarding knowledge ultimately erodes your power. If you know something very important, the way to get power is by actually sharing it."
– Joseph Badaracco

"You don't get to choose how you're going to die, or when. You can only decide how you're going to live. Now.
– Joan Baez

"There was such a difference, he thought, between the beauty that illuminated, and the beauty that was illuminated."
– R. Scott Bakker

"This ongoing journey requires faith in the power of a single lamp to hold the darkness at bay. It demands confidence in the power of humble actions to act as an inspiration, or a magnet, and draw in greater energies. There is also a need for a certain agility and strategic planning that puts these positive energies a few steps

ahead of the negative trends. And, above all, we need a constant awareness that the 'other' is not really different from the 'self.'"
– Rajni Bakshi

"Small mistakes tend to lead to large ones. Ours is a lifetime appointment, and all you have is your reputation. Once it's gone, it doesn't comeback."
– David Baldacci

"It is a terrible, an inexorable law that one cannot deny the humanity of another without diminishing one's own: in the face of one's victim, one sees oneself."
– James Baldwin

"Know from whence you came. If you know whence you came, there are absolutely no limitations to where you can go."
– James Baldwin

"It was books that taught me that the things that tormented me most were the very things that connected me with all the people who were alive, or who had ever lived."
– James Baldwin

"Never dull your shine for somebody else."
– Tyra Banks

"Though no one can go back and make a brand new start, anyone can start from now and make a brand new ending."
– Carl Bard

"To ignore the power of paradigms to influence your judgment is to put yourself at risk when exploring the future. To be able to shape your future, you have to be ready to change your paradigm."
– Joel Arthur Barker

"Dietary contributors to disease are easily swept aside, as our culture assumes it's normal to be chronically medicated to regulate cholesterol, blood pressure, and blood sugar."
– Neal Barnard

"Television is the first truly democratic culture — the first culture available to everybody and entirely governed by what the people want. The most terrifying thing is what people do want."
– Clive Barnes

"Connection with gardens, even small ones, even potted plants, can become windows to the inner life. The simple act of stopping and looking at the beauty around us can be prayer."
– Patricia R. Barret

"Those who bring sunshine into the lives of others cannot keep it from themselves."
– James M. Barrie

"You want to place blame on people, but I don't think it's fair. You're dealt the cards that you're dealt. You can let that be your downfall or a springboard to become something better. For me, I just thought, 'What a waste of time to be angry at my parents. What a waste of time to feel sorry for myself.' The best thing I can do is learn all the things I've learned from them, good and bad, have my own family someday, and just keep on

going. So many things are thrown at us as human beings, but you can't let any of them get you down, or you're just going to be defeated."
– Drew Barrymore

"All things splendid have been achieved by those who dared believe that something inside them was superior to circumstance."
– Bruce Barton

"I do not try to dance better than anyone else. I only try to dance better than myself."
– Mikhail Baryshnikov

"Sometimes you've got to be able to listen to yourself and be okay with no one else understanding."
– Christopher Barzak

"Every day is a journey, and the journey itself is home."
– Matsuo Basho

"Do not seek to follow in the footsteps of the wise. Seek what they sought."
– Matsuo Basho

"Look at the past as a bullet. Once it's fired it's finished."
– Catherine Bauby

"Someday the earth will weep, she will beg for her life, she will cry with tears of blood. You will make a choice, if you will help her or let her die, and when she dies, you too will die."
– Hollow Horn Bear

"Be daring, be different, be impractical, be anything that will assert integrity of purpose and imaginative vision against the play-it-safers, the creatures of the commonplace, the slaves of the ordinary."
– Cecil Beaton

"Live your life from your heart. Share from your heart. And your story will touch and heal people's souls."
– Melody Beattie

"Believe with all your heart that how you live your life makes a difference."
– Colin Beavan

"I really do think that any deep crisis is an opportunity to make your life extraordinary in some way."
– Martha Beck

"You cannot fix an illusion. You can only wake up from one."
– Michael Beckwith

"The mother's heart is the child's schoolroom."
– Henry Ward Beecher

"Storms purify the atmosphere."
– Henry Ward Beecher

"Every artist dips his brush in his own soul, and paints his own nature into his pictures."
– Henry Ward Beecher

"Don't only practice your art, but force your way into its secrets, for it and knowledge can raise men to the divine."
– Ludwig van Beethoven

"What is in my heart must come out, so I write it down."
– Ludwig Van Beethoven

"We are all too much inclined to walk through life with our eyes shut. There are things all around us, and right at our very feet, that we have never seen; because we have never really looked."
– Alexander Graham Bell

"Sometimes we stare so long at a door that is closing that we see too late the one that is open."
– Alexander Graham Bell

"Concentrate all your thoughts upon the work at hand. The sun's rays do not burn until brought to a focus."
– Alexander Graham Bell

"If one desires a change, one must be that change before that change can take place."
– Gita Bellin

"When people go to work, they shouldn't have to leave their hearts at home."
– Betty Bender

"All war represents a failure of diplomacy."
– Tony Benn

"To the artist is sometimes granted a sudden, transient insight which serves in this matter for experience. A flash, and where previously the brain held a dead fact, the soul grasps a living truth! At moments we are all artists."
– Arnold Bennett

"Everything that happens in all material, living, mental, or even spiritual processes involves the transformation of energy. Every thought, every sensation, every emotion is produced by energy exchanges."
– J. G. Bennett

"I'm strong on the outside, not all the way through. I've never been perfect, but neither have you."
– Chester Bennington

"If you want something you've never had, you have to do something you've never done."
– Kimnesha Benns

"Very often a change of self is needed more than a change of scene."
– AC Benson

"At the root of all power and motion, there is music and rhythm, the play of patterned frequencies against the matrix of time. We know that every particle in the physical universe takes its characteristics from the pitch and pattern and overtones of its particular frequencies, its singing. Before we make music, music makes us."
– Joachim-Ernst Berendt

"Don't let your habits become handcuffs."
– Elizabeth Berg

"Humiliation is one of the fastest ways to destroy the ego. Welcome moments of embarrassment as moments of accelerated change."
– Yehuda Berg

"Acknowledge all those who gave their lives in pursuit of the great human service, the service of the artist, transforming the sometimes unbearable discrepancy between the way things are and the way they ought to be, into something that makes us want to dance."
– Richard Berger

"The eye sees only what the mind is prepared to comprehend."
– Henri L. Bergson

"If opportunity doesn't knock, build a door."
– Milton Berle

"I'd rather be a could-be if I cannot be an are; because a could-be is a maybe who is reaching for a star. I'd rather be a has-been than a might-have-been, by far; for a might-have-been has never been, but a has was once an are."
– Milton Berle

"To understand is to perceive patterns."
– Isaiah Berlin

"Never assume that the guy understands that you and he have a relationship."
– Dave Berry

"You cannot devalue the body and value the soul — or value anything else. The isolation of the body sets it into direct conflict with everything else in creation."
– Wendell Berry

"If it's possible to build prison camps powerful enough to destroy human personalities, perhaps it was

also possible to create environments that can foster its rebirth."
– Bruno Bettelheim

"Life is raw material. We are artisans. We can sculpt our existence into something beautiful, or debase it into ugliness. It's in our hands."
– Cathy Better

"When you feel the suffering of every living thing in your own heart, that is consciousness."
– Bhagavad Gita

"The mind should dance with the body, and the whole universe is your stage. Try to feel that whatever you are doing is the most beautiful thing, the prettiest dance, because you are dancing with the whole universe. Don't resent anything. Let your heart guide you, free of all regimentation."
– Yogi Bhajan

"The courage to penetrate and power to see clearly the meaning of things hidden beyond the situation prevailing around us and to act up to the discovered meaning is what is known as revolutionary insight. Revolution can take place only where there is this power of penetrating insight."
– Vinoba Bhave

"I think I think, therefore I think I am."
– Ambrose Bierce

"Enjoy the journey, enjoy every moment, and quit worrying about winning and losing."
– Matt Biondi

"Dreams come in a size too big so that we may grow into them."
– Josie Bisset

"Don't you dare surround yourself with people who are not aware of the greatness that you are."
– Jo Blackwell-Preston

"Forgiveness is almost a selfish act because of its immense benefits to the one who forgives."
– Lawana Blackwell

"If the doors of perception were cleansed everything would appear to man as it is, infinite. For ma has closed himself up, till he sees all things through narrow chinks in his cavern."
– William Blake

"The man who never alters his opinion is like standing water, and breeds reptiles of the mind."
– William Blake

"What is now proved was once only imagined."
– William Blake

"There is between sleep and us something like a pact, a treaty with no secret clauses, and according to this convention it is agreed that, far from being a dangerous, bewitching force, sleep will become domesticated and serve as an instrument of our power to act. We surrender to sleep, but in the way that the master entrusts himself to the slave who serves him."
– Maurice Blanchot

"God made the world round so we would never be able to see too far down the road."
– Karen Blixen

"Education is the movement from darkness to light."
– Allan Bloom

"My only advice is to stay aware, listen carefully, and yell for help if you need it."
– Judy Blume

"Too many people realize at the end of their lives that they've taken for granted those who really love them."
– Lesley M.M. Blume

"Forgiveness does not change the past, but it does enlarge the future."
– Paul Boese

"Do not wait for leaders; do it alone, person to person."
– Anjeze Gonzhe "Mother Teresa" Bojaxhiu

"I am a little pencil in the hand of God who is writing a love letter to the world."
– Anjeze Gonzhe "Mother Teresa" Bojaxhiu

"Do not think that love, in order to be genuine, has to be extraordinary. What we need is to love without getting tired."
– Anjeze Gonzhe "Mother Teresa" Bojaxhiu

"Love is a fruit in season at all times, and within reach of every hand."
– Anjeze Gonzhe "Mother Teresa" Bojaxhiu

"If you judge people, you have no time to love them."
– Anjeze Gonzhe "Mother Teresa" Bojaxhiu

"There is more hunger for love and appreciation in this world than for bread."
– Anjeze Gonzhe "Mother Teresa" Bojaxhiu

"Be faithful in small things because it is in them that your strength lies."
– Anjeze Gonzhe "Mother Teresa" Bojaxhiu

"See how nature – trees, flowers, grass – grows in silence; see the stars, the moon and the sun, how they move in silence. We need silence to be able to touch souls."
– Anjeze Gonzhe "Mother Teresa" Bojaxhiu

"The first step to becoming is to will it."
– Anjeze Gonzhe "Mother Teresa" Bojaxhiu

"Be faithful in small things because it is in them that your strength lies."
– Anjeze Gonzhe "Mother Teresa" Bojaxhiu

"You have got to know what it is you want, or someone is going to sell you a bill of goods somewhere along the line that can do irreparable damage to your self-esteem, your sense of worth, and your stewardship of the talents that God gave you."
– Richard Nelson Bolles

"When I stand before God at the end of my life, I would hope that I would not have a single bit of talent left, and could say: I used everything you gave me."
– Erma Bombeck

"Silence in the face of evil is itself evil: God will not hold us guiltless.
Not to speak is to speak. Not to act is to act."
– Deitrich Bonhoeffer

"I have always imagined that paradise will be a kind of library."
– Jorge Luis Borges

"I think raising consciousness, helping people see and understand how they're connected to these larger systems in the world around us, is an incredibly important thing. I think art can do this in ways that are provocative, meaningful and inspirational, deeply moving, beautiful, connected with history and culture and resonant. I think that's a big part of it. There's another part of it where I think artists have the opportunity to more than call attention to problems and preach, to really help solve problems. To help create things that work better, that are just more beautiful and right."
– Sam Bower

"The more we accumulate wealth, the more it leads to a breakdown of community."
– Mark Boyle

"If we listened to our intellect we'd never have a love affair. We'd never have a friendship. We'd never go in business because we'd be cynical: 'It's gonna go wrong.' Or 'She's going to hurt me.' Or, 'I've had a couple of bad love affairs, so therefore . . .' Well, that's nonsense. You're going to miss life. You've got to jump off the cliff all the time and build your wings on the way down."
– Ray Bradbury

"The moment of enlightenment is when a person's dreams of possibilities become images of probabilities."
– Vic Braden

"I was told, 'You can be anything you want, kid.' When you hear that often enough, you believe it."
– Ed Bradley

"If we had no winter, the spring would not be so pleasant: if we did not sometimes taste of adversity, prosperity would not be so welcome."
– Anne Bradstreet

"If only I could throw away the urge to trace my patterns in your heart I could really see you."
– David Brandon

"There is overwhelming evidence that the higher the level of self-esteem, the more likely one will treat others with respect, kindness, and generosity. People who do not experience self-love have little or no capacity to love others."
– Nathanial Branden

"As for failures, I very, very rarely look back."
– Richard Branson

"Maybe you think you'll be entitled to more happiness later by forgoing all of it now, but it doesn't work that way. Happiness takes as much practice as unhappiness does. It's by living that you live more. By waiting you wait more. Every waiting day makes your life a little less. Every lonely day makes you a little smaller. Every day you put off your life makes you less capable of living it."
– Ann Brashares

"Enjoy the little things, for one day you may look back and realize they were the big things."
– Robert Brault

"Looking back, you realize that everything would have explained itself if you had only stopped interrupting."
– Robert Brault

"I know because I read…Your mind is not a cage. It's a garden. And it requires cultivating."
– Libba Bray

"I was motivated to be different in part because I was different."
– Donna Brazile

"Do not fear death so much, but rather the inadequate life."
– Bertolt Brecht

"Our goals can only be reached through a vehicle of a plan, in which we must fervently believe, and upon which we must vigorously act. There is no other route to success."
– Stephen A. Brennan

"Every time I close the door on reality, it comes in through the window."
– Ashleigh Brilliant

"A successful man is one who can lay a firm foundation with the bricks that others throw at him."
– David Brinkley

"It's the repetition of affirmations that leads to belief. And once that belief becomes a deep conviction, things begin to happen."
– Claude M. Bristol

"People are hungry for messages of hope and life."
– Morgan Brittany

"Temptation is not to be feared, but controlled."
– Deborah Brodie

"There is no happiness like that of being loved by your fellow creatures, and feeling that your presence is an addition to their comfort."
– Charlotte Bronte

"I'm happy to report that my inner child is still ageless."
– James Broughton

"Owning our story can be hard but not nearly as difficult as spending our lives running from it. Embracing our vulnerabilities is risky but not nearly as dangerous as giving up on love and belonging and joy—the experiences that make us the most vulnerable. Only when we are brave enough to explore the darkness will we discover the infinite power of our light."
– Brene Brown

"The more science I studied, the more I saw that physics becomes metaphysics and numbers become imaginary numbers. The farther you go into science, the mushier the ground gets. You start to say, 'Oh, there is an order and a spiritual aspect to science.'"
– Dan Brown

"Don't say you don't have enough time. You have exactly the same number of hours per day that were given to Helen Keller, Pasteur, Michaelangelo, Mother Teresa, Leonardo da Vinci, Thomas Jefferson, and Albert Einstein."
– H. Jackson Brown, Jr.

"Find a job you like and you add five days to every week."
– H. Jackson Brown, Jr.

"In the confrontation between the stream and the rock, the stream always wins – not through strength but by perseverance."
– H. Jackson Brown, Jr.

"The only true happiness comes from squandering ourselves for a purpose."
– John Mason Brown

"You don't have to be great to get started, but you have to get started to be great."
– Les Brown

"When you face your fear, most of the time you will discover that it was not really such a big threat after all. We all need some form of deeply rooted, powerful motivation – it empowers us to overcome obstacles so we can live our dreams."
– Les Brown

"Anyone who lives art knows that psychoanalysis has no monopoly on the power to heal. Art and poetry have always been altering our ways of sensing and feeling — that is to say, altering the human body."
– Norman O. Brown

"Complaining is not only hideously boring, but worse – it only increases the pain."
– Peter Megargee Brown

"Complaining is not only hideously boring, but worse – it only increases the pain."
– Peter Megargee Brown

"Creativity comes from trust. Trust your instincts. And never hope more than you work."
– Rita Mae Brown

"Language exerts hidden power, like a moon on the tides."
– Rita Mae Brown

"Creativity comes from trust. Trust your instincts."
– Rita Mae Brown

"When you've found another soul who see's in to your own, take good care of each other – and remember to be kind."
– Jackson Browne

"We carry within us the wonders we seek without us."
– Thomas Browne

"My sun sets to rise again."
– Robert Browning

"There are times when silence has the loudest voice."
– Leroy Brownlow

"Every day people are straying away from church and going back to God."
– Lenny Bruce

"The greatest things ever done on Earth have been done little by little."
– William Jennings Bryan

"People are lonely who build walls instead of bridges."
– Mark Buber

"The best things in life aren't things."
– Art Buchwald

"Truth is a demure lady, much too ladylike to knock you on the head and drag you to her cave. She is there, but the people must want her and seek her out."
– William F. Buckley, Jr.

"We are what we think. All that we are arises with our thoughts. With our thoughts we make our world."
– Gautama Buddha

"The way is not in the sky. The way is in the heart."
– Gautama Buddha

"All things appear and disappear because of the concurrence of causes and conditions. Nothing ever exists entirely alone; everything is in relation to everything else."
– Gautama Buddha

"The secret of health for both mind and body is not to mourn for the past, nor to worry about the future, but to live the present moment wisely and earnestly."
– Gautama Buddha

"The secret of health for both mind and body is not to mourn for the past, worry about the future, or anticipate troubles but to live in the present moment wisely and earnestly."
– Gautama Buddha

"All that we are is the result of what we have thought."
– Gautama Buddha

"You must be lamps unto yourselves."
– Gautama Buddha

"To keep the body in good health is a duty, otherwise we shall not be able to keep our mind strong and clear."
– Gautama Buddha

"The life I touch for good or ill will touch another life, and that in turn another, until who knows where the trembling stops or in what far place my touch will be felt."
– Frederick Buechner

"Once we recognize that all matter is actually energy, we can begin to form a new vision of ourselves and the world around us. We begin to realize that our surroundings are not what they seem."
– William Buhlman

"What you are is a question only you can answer."
– Lois McMaster Bujold

"When I begin to doubt my ability to work the word, I simply read another writer and know I have nothing to worry about. My contest is only with myself, to do it right, with power, and force, and delight, and gamble."
– Charles Bukowski

"Let us put our minds together and see what life we can make for our children."
– Sitting Bull

"I don't care what color you are, what sexual orientation you are, what nationality, what religion you are – if you operate out of a place of love, that's a family."
– Sandra Bullock

"To read without reflecting is like eating without digesting."
– Edmund Burke

"The grand essentials to happiness in this life are something to do, something to love, and something to hope for."
– George Washington Burnap

"Hang in there. It is astonishing how short a time it can take for very wonderful things to happen."
– Frances Hodgson Burnett

"The lure of the distant and the difficult is deceptive. The great opportunity is where you are."
– John Burroughs

"Desperation is the raw material of drastic change. Only those who can leave behind everything they have ever believed in can hope to escape."
– William S. Burroughs

"There are scores of people waiting for someone just like us to come along; people who will appreciate our compassion, our encouragement, who will need our unique talents. Someone who will live a happier life merely because we took the time to share what we had to give."
– Leo Buscaglia

"Love is always open arms. If you close your arms about love you will find that you are left holding only yourself."
– Leo Buscaglia

"There is a you, lying dormant. A potential within you to be realized. It does not matter whether you have an intelligence quotient of 60 or 160, there is more of you than what you are presently aware of. Perhaps the only peace and joy in life lies in the pursuit of and development of this potential."
– Leo Buscaglia

"If exercise could be packaged into a pill, it would be the single most prescribed and beneficial medicine in the nation."
– Robert Butler, M.D.

"Don't go through life. Grow through life."
– Eric Butterworth

"Prosperity is a way of living and thinking, and not just money or things. Poverty is a way of living and thinking, and not just a lack of money or things."
– Eric Butterworth

"The purpose of life is a life of purpose."
– Robert Byrne

"The best way to prepare for death is to live life to its fullest."
– John Bytheway

C

"When someone tells you that you can't do something, perhaps you should consider that they are only telling you what they can't do."
– Sheldon Cahoon

"There is zero correlation between being the best talker and having the best ideas."
– Susan Cain

"That is the difference between good teachers and great teachers: good teachers make the best of a pupil's means; great teachers foresee a pupil's ends."
– Maria Callas

"Find a place inside where there is joy, and the joy will burn out the pain."
– Joseph Campbell

"If you do follow your bliss you put yourself on a kind of track that has been there all the while, waiting for you, and the life that you ought to be living is the one you are living. Follow your bliss and don't be afraid, and doors will open where you didn't know they were going to be."
– Joseph Campbell

"Opportunities to find deeper powers within ourselves come when life seems most challenging."
– Joseph Campbell

"We don't realize that the gods are not out there somewhere. They live in us all. They are the energies of life itself.
– Joseph Campbell

"Real generosity toward the future lies in giving all to the present."
– Albert Camus

"Failure is the condiment that gives success its flavor."
– Truman Capote

"Life is much less a competitive struggle for survival than a triumph of cooperation and creativity."
– Fritjof Capra

"Think of how stupid the average person is, and realize half of them are stupider than that."
– George Carlin

"Never underestimate the power of stupid people in large groups."
– George Carlin

"Ask yourself this question: Will this matter a year from now?"
– Richard Carlson

"The man without a purpose is like a ship without a rudder – a waif, a nothing, a no man. Have a purpose in life, and having it, throw such strength of mind and muscle into your work as God has given you."
– Thomas Carlyle

"Silence is the element in which great things fashion themselves together."
– Thomas Carlyle

"As I grow older, I pay less attention to what men say. I just watch what they do."
– Andrew Carnegie

"Today is the tomorrow that you worried about yesterday."
– Dale Carnegie

"You have it easily in your power to increase the sum total of this world's happiness now. How? By giving a few words of sincere appreciation to someone who is lonely or discouraged. Perhaps you will forget tomorrow the kind words you say today, but the recipient may cherish them over a lifetime."
– Dale Carnegie

"It isn't what you have or who you are or where you are or what you are doing that makes you happy or unhappy. It is what you think about it."
– Dale Carnegie

"I think everybody should get rich and famous and do everything they ever dreamed of so they can see that it's not the answer."
– Jim Carrey

"Success is determined not by whether or not you face obstacles, but by your reaction to them. And if you look at these obstacles as a containing fence, they become your excuse for failure. If you look at them as a hurdle, each one strengthens you for the next."
– Ben Carson

"If you hear how wonderful you are often enough, you begin to believe it, no matter how you try to resist it."
– Ben Carson

"The human race is challenged more than ever before to demonstrate our mastery, not over nature but of ourselves."
– Rachel Carson

"Now I truly believe that we in this generation must come to terms with nature, and I think we're challenged, as mankind has never been challenged before, to prove our maturity and our mastery, not of nature but of ourselves."
– Rachel Carson

"Married men live longer than single men, but married men are a lot more willing to die."
– Johnny Carson

"The best measure of a human being is in how we treat the people who love us, and the people that we love."
– Lynda Carter

"If you doubt you can accomplish something, then you can't accomplish it. You have to have confidence in your ability, and then be tough enough to follow through."
– Rosalynn Carter

"Nothing is more beautiful than the woods before sunshine."
– George Washington Carver

"Most people search high and wide for the keys to success. If they only knew, the key to their dreams lies within."
– George Washington Carver

"In music, in the sea, in a flower, in a leaf, in an act of kindness. I see what people call God in all these things."
– Pablo Casals

"Each person has inside a basic decency and goodness. If he listens to it and acts on it, he is giving a great deal of what it is the world needs most. It is not complicated but it takes courage. It takes courage for a person to listen to his own goodness and act on it."
– Pablo Casals

"Resilience is all about being able to overcome the unexpected. Sustainability is about survival. The goal of resilience is to thrive."
– Jamais Cascio

"No matter how old you get, if you can keep the desire to be creative, you're keeping the man-child alive."
– John Cassavetes

"Give me strength, not to be better than my enemies, but to defeat my greatest enemy, the doubts within myself. Give me strength for a straight back and clear eyes, so when life fades, as the setting sun, my spirit may come to you without shame."
– P.C. Cast

"Remember, darkness does not always equate to evil, just as light does not always bring good."
– P.C. Cast

"Human beings are perceivers, but the world they perceive is an illusion created by the description that was told to them from the moment they were born."
– Carlos Castenada

"We either make ourselves happy or miserable. The amount of work is the same."
– Carlos Castaneda

"Self-importance is our greatest enemy. Think about it – what weakens us is feeling offended by the deeds and misdeeds of our fellowmen. Our self-importance requires that we spend most of our lives offended by someone."
– Carlos Castaneda

"I feel even more beautiful at 105 than I did at 104."
– Panchita Castillo

"Every artist makes herself born. You must bring the artist into the world yourself."
– Willa Cather

"Where there is great love there are always miracles."
– Willa Cather

"As long as people will accept crap, it will be financially profitable to dispense of it."
– Dick Cavett

"Tell me thy company, and I will tell thee what thou art."
– Miquel de Cervantes

"If through a broken heart God can bring His purposes to pass in the world, then thank Him for breaking your heart."
– Oswald Chambers

"Each of us is meant to have a character all our own, to be what no other can exactly be, and do what no other can exactly do."
– William Ellery Channing

"The worst tyrants are those which establish themselves in our own breasts."
– William Ellery Channing

"Do not judge from mere appearances; for the lift laugher that bubbles on the lip often mantles over the depths of sadness, and the serious look may be the sober veil that covers a divine peace and joy. The bosom can ache beneath diamond brooches; and many a blithe heart dances under coarse wool."
– Edwin Hubble Chapin

"Every action in our lives touches on some chord that will vibrate in eternity."
– Edwin Hubbel Chapin

"Never does the human soul appear so strong as when it forgoes revenge, and dares forgive an injury."
– Edwin Hubbel Chapin

"Nothing is permanent in this wicked world, not even our troubles."
– Charles Chaplin

"You'll never find a rainbow if you're looking down"
– Charles Chaplin

"Being in love shows a person who he should be."
– Anton Chekhov

"A dead thing goes with the stream, but only a living thing can go against it."
– G.K. Chesterton

"There is the great lesson of 'Beauty and the Beast,' that a thing must be loved before it is lovable."
– G.K. Chesterton

"There is a road from the eye to the heart that does not go through the intellect."
– G.K. Chesterton

"A common conception of security is an achievement or possession on the physical plane. But an abiding sense of security can never come from possession or from achievement. Security comes only when we have established our constant oneness with our soul."
– Sri Chinmoy

"When you begin to touch your heart or let your heart be touched, you begin to discover that it's bottomless."
– Pema Chodron

"It's pretty irionic that the so-called 'least advantaged' people are the ones taking the lead in trying to protect all of us, while the richest and most powerful among us are the ones who are trying to drive the society to destruction."
– Noam Chomsky

"If we just shook and rattled the old chains, nothing would move. One must add one's own link to the chain. The more original the link, the greater the step forward."
– Frederic Chopin

"If you seek love, appreciation, and affection, then learn to give love, appreciation, and affection."
– Deepak Chopra

"If we just shook and rattled the old chains, nothing would move. One must add one's own link to the chain. The more original the link, the greater the step forward."
– Frederic Chopin

"It is never too late, you are never too sick, and you are never too old to start from scratch once again."
– Bikram Choudhury

"Peace I leave with you, my peace I give unto you: not as the world giveth, give I unto you. Let not your heart be troubled, neither let it be afraid."
– Jesus Christ

"The freedom of every artist is essential."
– Christo

"It is not whether your words or actions are tough or gentle; it is the spirit behind your actions and words that announces your inner state."
– Chin-Ning Chu

"Continuous effort – not strength or intelligence – is the key to unlocking our potential."
– Winston Churchill

"To each there comes in their lifetime a special moment when they are figuratively tapped on the shoulder and offered the chance to do a very special thing, unique to them and fitted to their talents. What a tragedy if that moment finds them unprepared or unqualified for that which could have been their finest hour."
– Winston Churchill

"No matter who you are, no matter what you did, no matter where you've come from, you can always change, become a better version of yourself."
– Madonna Louise Ciccone

"Poor is the man whose pleasures depend on the permission of another."
– Madonna Louise Ciccone

"I am my own experiment. I am my own work of art."
– Madonna Louise Ciccone

"The people's good is the highest law."
– Marcus Tullius Cicero

"A man of courage is also full of faith."
– Marcus Tullius Cicero

"Nature has planted in our minds an insatiable longing to see the truth."
– Marcus Tullius Cicero

"To some extent, I liken slavery to death."
– Marcus Tullius Cicero

"I think that's what our world is desperately in need of – lovers, people who are building deep, genuine relationships with fellow strugglers along the way, and who actually know the faces of the people behind the issues they are concerned about."
– Shane Claiborne

"We've put more effort into helping folks reach old age than in helping them enjoy it."
– Frank A. Clark

"We are each so much more than what some reduce to measuring."
– Karen Kaiser Clark

"Our duty is wakefulness, the fundamental condition of life itself. The unseen, the unheard, the untouchable is what weaves the fabric of our see-able universe together."
– Robin Craig Clark

"Now here's the thing about being a little off-center; you're never sure if you're a bona fide loon or if you have insight that other people don't have. You have to navigate through life using a kind of psychic gyroscope to keep from falling too far one way or another, and you feel a peculiar kinship with other people who are also a little bit off-center."
– Blaize Clement

"Wanting to be someone you're not is a waste of the person you are."
– Kurt Cobain

"The duty of youth is to challenge corruption."
– Kurt Cobain

"It's better to be hated for what you are than to be loved for what you aren't."
– Kurt Cobain

"To enjoy being famous, you need to have a screw loose."
– Diablo Cody

"No matter what he does, every person on earth plays a central role in the history of the world. And normally he doesn't know it."
– Paulo Coelho

"You will never be able to escape from your heart. So it's better to listen to what it has to say."
– Paulo Coelho

"It's the possibility of having a dream come true that makes life interesting."
– Paulo Coelho

"It takes a lot of courage to release the familiar and seemingly secure, to embrace the new. But there is no real security in what is no longer meaningful. There is more security in the adventurous and exciting, for in movement there is life, and in change there is power."
– Alan Cohen

"Luck is what you have left over after you give 100 percent."
– Langston Coleman

"Advice is like snow; the softer it falls, the longer it dwells upon, and the deeper it sinks into the mind."
– Samuel Taylor Coleridge

"What a wonderful life I've had! I only wish I'd realized it sooner."
– Colette

"Be happy. It's one way of being wise."
– Sidonie-Gabrielle Colette

"There's nothing wrong with you. There's a lot wrong with the world you live in. And definitely get out of high school and make everyone sorry."
– Chris Colfer

"Visualize this thing you want. See it, feel it, believe in it. Make your mental blueprint and begin."
– Robert Collier

"Aim higher in case you fall short."
– Suzanne Collins

"He that to what he sees, adds observation, and to what he reads, reflection, is in the right road to knowledge."
– Caleb Colton

"Behold the turtle. He makes progress only when he sticks his neck out."
– James Bryant Conant

"Our greatest glory is not in never falling, but in rising every time we fall."
– Confucius

"Respect yourself and others will respect you."
– Confucius

"Courtship is to marriage, as a very witty prologue to a very dull play."
– William Congreve

"I think the act of reading imbues the reader with a sensitivity toward the outside world that people who don't read can sometimes lack. I know it seems like a contradiction in terms; after all reading is such a solitary, internalizing act that it appears to represent a disengagement from day-to-day life. But reading, and particularly the reading of fiction, encourages us to view the world in new and challenging ways...It allows us to inhabit the consciousness of another which is a precursor to empathy, and empathy is, for me, one of the marks of a decent human being."
– John Connolly

"The question is not how to get cured, but how to live."
– Joseph Conrad

"Our deepest roots are in nature. No matter who we are, where we live, or what kind of life we lead, we remain irrevocably linkes with the rest of Creation."
– Charles Cook

"It all depends on whether you have things, or they have you."
– Robert Cook

"Grace is the face that love wears when it meets imperfection."
– Joseph R. Cooke

"Middle age went by while I was mourning for my lost youth."
– Mason Cooley

"An artist is not a special kind of a person — every person is a special kind of an artist."
– Ananda Coomaraswami

"The most important thing in life is to stop saying 'I wish' and start saying 'I will.' Consider nothing impossible, then treat possibilities as probabilities."
– David Copperfield

"Do no harm & leave the world a better place than you found it."
– Patricia Cornwell

"Family is conflict, and it is something we all relate to."
– Bill Cosby

"We're afraid of a lot of things in life. It's part of the human condition. What do we fear? Love? Failure? Telling the truth about ourselves? I think we don't show people all we truly are because we're afraid that if they actually know everything about us, they won't love us. I'm as guilty of that as anyone."
– Kevin Costner

"Nothing is more powerful than an individual acting out of his conscience, thus helping to bring the collective conscience to life."
– Norman Cousins

"It is well known that panic, despair, depression, hate, rage, exasperation, frustration all produce negative biochemical changes in the body."
– Norman Cousins

"If we were logical, the future would be bleak indeed. But we are more than logical. We are human beings, and we have faith, and we have hope, and we can work."
– Jacques Cousteau

"Happiness depends, as Nature shows, less on exterior things than most suppose."
– William Cowper

"Live out of your imagination, not your history."
– Stephen R. Covey

"No one knows your capability as well as you do. No one knows how big you can dream and no one knows how far you can go. You, like water, can seek and reach your own level."
– Lynne Cox

"Most people think happiness is about gaining something, but it's not. It's all about getting rid of the darkness you accumulate."
– Carolyn Crane

"Be careful with the present you are creating – it should look like the future you dream of."
– Mujeres Creando

"Gratitude is something of which none of us can give too much. For on the smiles, the thanks we give, our little gestures of appreciation, our neighbors build their philosophy of life."
– A. J. Cronin

"Real courage is doing the right thing when nobody's looking. Doing the unpopular thing because it's what you believe, and the heck with everybody."
– Justin Cronin

"The whole culture is one unified field of bought, sold, market researched everything. It used to be that people fermented their own culture. It took hundreds of years and it evolved over time. That's gone in America. People now don't have any concept that there ever was a culture outside this thing that's created to make money. Whatever is the biggest, latest thing, they're into it. You just get disgusted after a while for not having more of a kind of like intellectual curiosity about what's behind all this jive bullshit."
– Robert Dennis Crumb

"You have to love dancing to stick to it. It gives you nothing back, no manuscripts to store away, no paintings to show on walls and maybe hang in museums, no poems to be printed and sold, nothing but that single fleeting moment when you feel alive."
– Merce Cunningham

"Life is not easy for any of us. But what of that? We must have perseverance and above all confidence in ourselves. We must believe that we are gifted for something and that this thing must be attained."
– Marie Curie

"Things will change: you won't feel this way forever. And anyway, sometimes the hardest lessons to learn are the ones your soul needs most."
– Kelly Cutrone

"I advise you to stop sharing your dreams with people who try to hold you back, even if they're your parents. Because, if you're the kind of person who senses there's something out there for you beyond whatever it is you're expected to do – if you want to be extra-ordinary you will not get there by hanging around a bunch of people who tell you you're not extraordinary. Instead, you will probably become as ordinary as they expect you to be."

– Kelly Cutrone

D

"A little nonsense now and then is relished by the wisest men."
– Roald Dahl

"Each morning when I awake, I experience again a supreme pleasure: that of being Salvador Dali."
– Salvador Dali

"If you have time to whine and complain about something, then you have the time to do something about it."
– Anthony J. D'Angelo

"One life is all we have and we live it as we believe in living it. But to sacrifice what you are and to live without belief, that is a fate more terrible than dying."
– Jeanne d'Arc

"A man who dares to waste one hour of time has not discovered the value of life."
– Charles Darwin

"No one can stand in these solitudes unmoved, and not feel that there is more in man than the mere breath of his body."
– Charles Darwin

"If the misery of the poor be caused not by the laws of nature, but by our institutions, great is our sin."
– Charles Darwin

"It is not the strongest of the species that survive, nor the most intelligent, but the most responsive to change."
– Charles Darwin

"The shadow is the greatest teacher for how to come to the light."
– Ram Dass

"The shadow is the greatest teacher for how to come to the light."
– Ram Dass

"Only that in you which is me can hear what I'm saying."
– Ram Dass

"I have been impressed with the urgency of doing. Knowing is not enough; we must apply. Being willing is not enough; we must do."
– Leonardo da Vinci

"Water is the driving force of nature."
– Leonardo da Vinci

"Water is to the world as blood is to our bodies."
– Leonardo da Vinci

"Obstacles cannot crush me. Every obstacle yields to stern resolve. He who is fixed to a star does not change his mind."
– Leonardo da Vinci

"Once you have tasted flight, you will forever walk the earth with your eyes turned skyward, for there you have been, and there you will always long to return."
– Leonardo da Vinci

"Nature never breaks her own laws."
– Leonardo da Vinci

"Simplicity is the ultimate sophistication."
– Leonardo da Vinci

"We have all known the long loneliness and we have learned that the only solution is love and that love comes with community."
– Dorothy Day

"What else is the world interested in? What else do we all want, each one of us, except to love and be loved, in our families, in our work, in all our relationships?"
– Dorothy Day

"I am opposing a social order in which it is possible for one man who does absolutely nothing that is useful to amass a fortune of hundreds of millions of dollars, while millions of men and women who work all the days of their lives secure barely enough for a wretched existence."
– Eugene Debs

"Being a Baptist won't keep you from sinning, but it'll sure as hell keep you from enjoying it."
– James Dean

"Only the gentle are ever really strong."
– James Dean

"Love may be or it may not, but where it is, it ought to reveal itself in its immensity."
– Honore de Balzac

"It is one of the unexpected disasters of the modern age that our new unparalleled access to information has come at the price of our capacity to concentrate on anything much."
– Alain de Botton

"Work finally beings when the fear of doing nothing exceeds the fear of doing it badly."
– Alain de Botton

"Take away the cause, and the effect ceases."
– Miguel de Cervantes

"You are not a human being in search of a spiritual experience. You are a spiritual being immersed in a human experience."
– Pierre Teilhard de Chardin

"We are one, after all, you and I. Together we suffer, together exist, and forever will recreate each other."
– Pierre Teilhard de Chardin

"The kind of beauty I want most is the hard-to-get kind that comes from within - strength, courage, dignity."
– Ruby Dee

"When you take risks you learn that there will be times when you succeed and there will be times when you fail, and both are equally important."
– Ellen DeGeneres

"Follow your passion. Stay true to yourself. Never follow someone else's path unless you're in the woods and you're lost and you see a path. By all means, you should follow that."
– Ellen DeGeneres

"You should never assume. You know what happens when you assume. You make an ass out of you and me because that's how it's spelled."
– Ellen DeGeneres

"I expect to pass through this world but once; any good thing therefore that I can do, or any kindness that I can show to any fellow creature, let me do it now; let me not defer or neglect it, for I shall not pass this way again."
– Etienne de Grellet

"Music is the literature of the heart; it commences where speech ends."
– Alphonse de Lamartine

"It is incontestable that music induces in us a sense of the infinite and the contemplation of the invisible."
– Victor de LaPrade

"We should not judge a man's merit by his great abilities, but by the use he makes of them."
– François de la Rochefoucauld

"We are nearer loving those who hate use than those who love us more than we wish."
– Francois de La Rochefoucauld

"I don't want to live in the kind of world where we don't look out for each other. Not just the people that are close to us, but anybody who needs a helping hand. I cant change the way anybody else thinks, or what they choose to do, but I can do my bit."
– Charles de Lint

"Distance sometimes lets you know who's worth keeping and who's worth letting go."
– Lana Del Rey

"Most of us serve our ideals by fits and starts. The person who makes a success of living is the one who sees his goal steadily and aims for it unswervingly. That is dedication."
– Cecil B. De Mille

"The wrongdoer is more unfortunate than the man wronged."
– Democritus

"The great and glorious masterpiece of humanity is to know how to live with a purpose."
– Michel Eyquem de Montaigne

"I like being famous when it's convenient for me, and completely anonymous when it's not."
– Catherine Deneuve

"If you don't like seeing pictures of violence towards animals being posted, you need to help stop the violence, not the pictures."
– Johnny Depp

"In the end, it is important to remember that we cannot become what we need to be, by remaining what we are."
– Max DePree

"We cannot become what we want to be by remaining what we are."
– Max DePree

"The most beautiful things in the world cannot be seen or touched, they are felt with the heart."
– Antoine de Saint-Exupery

"I have no right to say or do anything that diminishes a man in his own eyes. What matters is not what I think of him but what he thinks of himself. Hurting a man in his dignity is a crime."
– Antoine de Saint-Exupery

"If you want to build a ship, don't herd people together to collect wood and don't assign them tasks and work, but rather teach them to long for the endless immensity of the sea."
– Antoine de Saint-Exupery

"I know but one freedom and that is the freedom of the mind."
– Antoine de Saint-Exupery

"A rock pile ceases to be a rock pile the moment a single man contemplates it, bearing within him the image of a cathedral."
– Antoine de Saint-Exupery

"You should never be surprised when someone treats you with respect, you should expect it."
– Sarah Dessen

"The further you go, the more you have to be proud of. At the same time, in order to come a long way, you have to be behind to begin with. IN the end, though maybe it's not how you reach a place that matters. Just that you get there at all."
– Sarah Dessen

"Anyone can hide. Facing up to things, working through them, that's what makes you strong."
– Sarah Dessen

"Keep your dreams alive. Understand to achieve anything requires faith and belief in yourself, vision, hard work, determination, and dedication. Remember all things are possible for those who believe."
– Gail Devers

"Noble and great. Courageous and determined. Faithful and fearless. That is who you are and who you have always been. And understanding it can change your life, because this knowledge carries a confidence that cannot be duplicated any other way."
– Sheri L. Dew

"To maintain the state of doubt and to carry on systematic and protracted inquiry – these are the essentials of thinking."
– John Dewey

"Healing is communication; and music, in its universal nature, is total communication. In the deepest mysteries of music are the inspirations, the pathways, and the healing which lead to one-ness and unity."
– Olivea Dewhurst-Maddock

"In much of the rest of the world, rich people live in gated communities and drink bottled water. That's increasingly the case in Los Angeles where I come from. So that wealthy people in much of the world are insulated from the consequences of their actions."
– Jared Diamond

"You can't always judge people by the things they done. You got to judge them by what they are doing now."
– Kate DiCamillo

"I never could have done what I have done without the habits of punctuality, order, and diligence, without the determination to concentrate myself on one subject at a time."
– Charles Dickens

"Reflect upon your present blessings, of which every man has plenty; not on your past misfortunes, of which all men have some."
– Charles Dickens

"To live is so startling it leaves little time for anything else."
– Emily Dickinson

"The soul should always stand ajar, ready to welcome the ecstatic experience."
– Emily Dickinson

"That is will never come again is what makes life so sweet."
– Emily Dickinson

"Hope is the thing with feathers that perches in the soul and sings the tune without words and never stops at all."
– Emily Dickinson

"To free us from the expectations of others, to give us back to ourselves — there lies the great, singular power of self-respect."
– Joan Didion

"Character – the willingness to accept responsibility for one's own life – is the source from which self-respect springs."
– Joan Didion

"The willingness to accept responsibility for one's own life is the source from which self-respect springs."
– Joan Didion

"You do not have to sit outside in the dark. If, however, you want to look at the stars, you will find that darkness is necessary. But the stars neither require nor demand it."
– Annie Dillard

"Housework can't kill you, but why take a chance?"
– Phyllis Diller

"Never go to bed mad. Stay up and fight."
– Phyllis Diller

"Whey worry? If you've done the very best you can, worrying won't make it any better."
– Walt Disney

"Most people die with their music still locked up inside them."
– Banjamin Disraeli

"Action may not always bring happiness, but there is no happiness without action."
– Benjamin Disraeli

"The greatest good you can do for another is not just to share your riches but to reveal to him his own."
– Benjamin Disraeli

"Every production of genius must be the production of enthusiasm."
– Benjamin Disraeli

"Nurture your mind with great thoughts, for you will never go any higher than your thoughts."
– Benjamin Disraeli

"You're never a loser until you quit trying."
– Mike Ditka

"Habits of the mind also provide our mental framework: the way we see the world."
– Gyalwa Dokhampa

"You can tell the ideals of a nation by its advertisements."
– Norman Douglass

"If you want to be respected by others the great thing is to respect yourself. Only by that, only by self respect will you compel others to respect you."
– Fyodor Dostoyevsky

"Happiness does not lie in happiness, but in the achievement of it."
– Fyodor Dostoyevsky

"Lying to ourselves is more deeply ingrained than lying to others."
– Fyodor Dostoyevsky

"Whatever you persistently allow to occupy your thoughts will magnify in your life."
– Frederick Douglass

"It is easier to build strong children than to repair broken men."
– Frederick Douglass

"You have the power to choose your own happiness. People, situations, and events outside of yourself will affect you, but no one can give you happiness."
– Stephanie Dowrick

"There are heroisms all round us waiting to be done."
– Arthur Conan Doyle

"The core psychology of a social entrepreneur is someone who cannot come to rest, in a very deep sense, until he or she has changed the pattern in an area of social concern all across society."
– Bill Drayton

"The best way to predict the future is to create it."
– Peter F. Drucker

"Unless commitment is made, there are only promises and hopes; but no plans."
– Peter F. Drucker

"Knowledge has to be improved, challenged, and increased constantly, or it vanishes."
– Peter F. Drucker

"The important thing is this: to be ready at any moment to sacrifice what you are for what you could become."
– Charles DuBois

"The important thing is this: To be able at any moment to sacrifice what we are for what we could become."
– Charles DuBois

"Artmaking is making the invisible, visible."
– Marcel Duchamp

"I don't believe in hate. To me it wastes too much time. People who hate waste so much of their life hating that they miss out on all the other stuff out here."
– Jaycee Dugard

"Live every day to the fullest, whatever life brings you."
– Jaycee Dugard

"You don't get old until you replace dreams with regrets."
– Troy Dumais

"When you judge another, you do not define them, you define yourself."
– Wayne Dyer

"May you grow up to be righteous, may you grow up to be true. May you always know the truth and see the lights surrounding you."
– Bob Dylan

"He not busy being born is busy dying."
– Bob Dylan

E

"No kind action ever stops with itself. One kind action leads to another. Good example is followed. A single act of kindness throws out roots in all directions, and the roots spring up and make new trees. The greatest work that kindness does to others is that it makes them kind themselves."
– Amelia Earhart

"What we plant in the soil of contemplation, we shall reap in the harvest of action.
– Meister Eckhart

"Education is for improving the lives of others and for leaving your community and world better than you found it."
– Marian Wright Edelman

"If we don't stand up for children, then we don't stand for much."
– Marian Wright Edelman

"We must not, in trying to think about how we can make a big difference, ignore the small daily differences we can make which, over time, add up to big differences that we often cannot foresee."
– Marian Wright Edelman

"There is no supernatural. We are continually learning new things. There are powers within us which have not yet been developed and they will develop. We shall learn things of ourselves, which will be full of wonders, but none of them will be beyond the natural.
– Thomas Edison

"The doctor of the future will give no medicine but will interest his patients in the care of the human frame, in diet, and in the cause and prevention of disease."
– Thomas Alva Edison

"Opportunity is missed by most people because it comes dressed in overalls and looks like work."
– Thomas Alva Edison

"Once you start to see through the myth of status, possessions, and unlimited consumption as a path to happiness, you'll find that you have all kinds of freedom and time. It's like a deal you can make with the universe:

I'll give up greed for freedom. Then you can start putting your time to good use."
– David Edwards

"She stood in the storm, and when the wind did not blow her away, she adjusted her sails."
– Elizabeth Edwards

"We must teach our children to dream with their eyes open."
– Harry Edwards

"Sometimes, as we're stumbling along in the dark, we hit something good."
– Susan Ee

"If you want success and wealth, then stop spending too much time on cyber world."
– Ehabib

"Avoid loud and aggressive persons, they are vexations to the spirit."
– Max Ehrmann

"With all its sham, drudgery, and broken dreams, it is still a beautiful life."
– Max Ehrmann

"Exercise caution in your business affairs, for the world is full of trickery. But let not this blind you to what virtue there is; many persons strive for high ideals, and everywhere life is full of heroism. Be yourself. Especially do not feign affection. Neither be cynical about love; for in the face of all aridity and disenchantment it is as perennial as the grass. Take kindly the counsel of the years, gracefully surrendering the things of youth.
– Max Ehrmann

"Go placidly amid the noise and the haste, and remember what peace there may be in silence. As far as possible without surrender, be on good terms with all persons. Speak your truth quietly and clearly, and listen to others, even the dull and ignorant; they too have their story. Be yourself. Especially do not feign affection. Neither be cynical about love – for in the face of all aridity and disenchantment is it perennial as the grass. Take kindly the counsel of the years, gracefully surrendering the things of youth. Nurture strength of spirit to shield you from misfortune. But do not distress yourself with imaginings. Many fears are born of fatigue and loneliness. Beyond a wholesome discipline, be gentle with yourself. You are a child of the universe no less than the trees and the stars; you have a right to be here. And whether or not it is clear to you, no doubt the universe is unfolding as it should. Therefore be at peace with God, whatever you conceive Him to be, and whatever your labours and aspirations, in the noisy confusion of life keep peace with your soul. With all its sham, drudgery and broken dreams, it is still a beautiful world."
– Max Ehrmann

"With all its sham, drudgery, and broken dreams, it is still a beautiful life."
– Max Ehrmann

"Intellectual growth should commence at birth and cease only at death."
– Albert Einstein

"A new type of thinking is essential if mankind is to survive and move towards higher levels."
– Albert Einstein

"Learn from yesterday, live for today, hope for tomorrow."
– Albert Einstein

"In the middle of difficulty lies opportunity."
– Albert Einstein

"Everyone should be respected as an individual, but no one idolized."
– Albert Einstein

"If you want your children to be intelligent, read them fairy tales."
– Albert Einstein

"Once you stop learning, you start dying."
– Albert Einstein

"If people are good only because they fear punishment and hope for reward, then we are a sorry lot indeed."
– Albert Einstein

"Everyone is a genius. But, if you judge a fish on its ability to climb a tree, it will live its whole life believing that it is stupid."
– Albert Einstein

"Try not to become a man of success. Rather, become a man of value."
– Albert Einstein

"If you want your children to be intelligent, read them fairy tales."
– Albert Einstein

"Once you stop learning, you start dying."
– Albert Einstein

"If people are good only because they fear punishment and hope for reward, then we are a sorry lot indeed."
– Albert Einstein

"The value of achievement lies in the achieving."
– Albert Einstein

"When you examine the lives of the most influential people who have ever walked among us, you discover one thread that winds through them all. They have been aligned first with their spiritual nature and only then with their physical selves."
– Albert Einstein

"A human being is a part of the whole, called by us, 'Universe,' a part limited in time and space. He experiences himself, his thoughts and feelings as something separated from the rest — a kind of optical delusion of his consciousness.

This delusion is a kind of prison for us, restricting us to our personal desires and to affection for a few persons nearest to us. Our task must be to free ourselves from this prison by widening our circle of compassion to embrace all living creatures and the whole of nature in its beauty.

Nobody is able to achieve this completely, but the striving for such achievement is in itself a part of the liberation and a foundation for inner security."
– Albert Einstein

"Your imagination is the preview of life's coming attractions."
– Albert Einstein

"Three rules of work: Out of clutter find simplicity; From discord find harmony; In the middle of difficulty lies opportunity."
– Albert Einstein

"The only thing that interferes with my learning is my education."
– Albert Einstein

"It is a miracle that curiosity survives formal education."
– Albert Einstein

"The world is a dangerous place, not because of those who do evil, but because of those who look on and do nothing."
– Albert Einstein

"The most beautiful experience we can have is the mysterious — the fundamental emotion which stands at the cradle of true art and true science."
– Albert Einstein

"The problems we have today will not be solved by thinking the way we thought when we created them."
– Albert Einstein

"All meaningful and lasting change starts first in your imagination and then works its way out."
– Albert Einstein

"If I were not a physicist, I would probably be a musician. I often think in music. I live my daydreams in music. I see my life in terms of music."
– Albert Einstein

"Nationalism is an infantile disease. It is the measles of mankind."
– Albert Einstein

"No problem can be solved from the same level of consciousness that created it."
– Albert Einstein

"In the middle of difficulty lies opportunity."
– Albert Einstein

"My position concerning God is that of an agnostic. I am convinced that a vivid consciousness of the primary importance of moral principles for the betterment and ennoblement of life does not need the idea of a law-giver, especially a law-giver who works on the basis of reward and punishment."
– Albert Einstein

"Whoever undertakes to set himself up as judge of truth and knowledge is shipwrecked by the laughter of the gods."
– Albert Einstein

"I believe in Spinoza's God, who reveals Himself in the lawful harmony of the world, not in a God who concerns Himself with the fate and the doings of mankind."
– Albert Einstein

"The ideals that have lighted my way, and time after time have given me new courage to face life cheerfully, have been kindness, beauty, and truth."
– Albert Einstein

"Great spirits have always encountered violent opposition from mediocre minds."
– Albert Einstein

"A hundred times every day I remind myself that my inner and outer life are based on the labor of others, living and dead, and that I must exert myself in order to give in the same measure as I have received and am receiving."
– Albert Einstein

"There are only two ways to live your life. One is as though nothing is a miracle. The other is as though everything is a miracle."
– Albert Einstein

"Make friends with your shower. If inspired to sing, maybe the song has an idea in it for you."
– Albert Einstein

"The pursuit of truth and beauty is a sphere of activity in which we are permitted to remain children all our lives."
– Albert Einstein

"Small is the number of them that see with their own eyes and feel with their own hearts."
– Albert Einstein

"Art is literacy of the heart."
– Elliot Eisner

"To maintain a skillful balance between the inner and outer aspects of our lives is an enormously challenging and continuously changing process. The objective is not to dogmatically live with less, but is a more demanding intention of living with balance in order to find a life of greater purpose, fulfillment, and satisfaction."
– Duane Elgin

"Deep unspeakable suffering may well be called a baptism, a regeneration, the initiation into a new state."
– George Eliot

"It is never too late to be what we might have been."
– George Eliot

"For last year's words belong to last year's language. And next year's words await another voice. What we call the beginning is often the end. And to make an end is to make a beginning."
– T. S. Eliot

"What do we live for, if it is not to make life less difficult for each other?"
– George Eliot

"We must not cease from exploration; the end of all our exploring will be to arrive where we began and to know the place for the first time."
– T. S. Eliot

"Power is strength and the ability to see yourself through your own eyes and not through the eyes of another. It is being able to place a circle of power at your own feet and not take power from someone else's circle."
– Agnes Whistling Elk

"Sometimes you have to steer away from the crowd in order to be a better person. It's not always easy, that's for sure. But it's right. And sometimes doing the right thing feels good, even if it does end up in a trip to the principal's office."
– Simone Elkeles

"A problem is a chance for you to do your best."
– Duke Ellington

"By being yourself you put something wonderful in the world that was not there before."
– Edwin Elliot

"People got insights into what was bothering them, but they hardly did a damn thing to change."
– Albert Ellis

"All the art of living lies in a fine mingling of letting go and holding on."
– Havelock Ellis

"I was never more hated than when I tried to be honest. Or when, even as just now I've tried to articulate exactly what I felt to be the truth. No one was satisfied."
– Ralph Ellison

"Envy is ignorance, imitation is suicide."
– Ralph Waldo Emerson

"Earth laughs in flowers."
– Ralph Waldo Emerson

"Truth is the property of no individual, but is the treasure of all men."
– Ralph Waldo Emerson

"Let me never fall into the vulgar mistake of dreaming that I am persecuted whenever I am contradicted."
– Ralph Waldo Emerson

"Let us be silent, that we may hear the whispers of the gods."
– Ralph Waldo Emerson

"The only person you are destined to become is the person you decide to be."
– Ralph Waldo Emerson

"What lies behind us and what lies before us are tiny matters compared to what lies within us. And when we bring what is within out into the world, miracles happen."
– Ralph Waldo Emerson

"Be not the slave of your own past — plunge into the sublime seas, dive deep, and swim far, so you shall come back with self-respect, with new power, with an advanced experience, that shall explain and overlook the old."
– Ralph Waldo Emerson

"Most of the shadows of this life are caused by standing in one's own sunshine."
– Ralph Waldo Emerson

"To be yourself in a world that is constantly trying to make you something else is the greatest accomplishment."
– Ralph Waldo Emerson

"Skill to do comes of doing."
– Ralph Waldo Emerson

"Do not follow where the path may lead. Go instead where there is no path and create a trail."
– Ralph Waldo Emerson

"If the stars should appear but one night every thousand years how man would marvel and adore."
– Ralph Waldo Emerson

"I fear the popular notion of success stands in direct opposition in all points to the real and wholesome success. One adores public opinion, the other, private opinion; one, fame, the other, desert; one, feats, the other, humility; one, lucre, the other, love."
– Ralph Waldo Emerson

"Concentration is the secret of strength."
– Ralph Waldo Emerson

"Be an opener of doors for such as come after thee."
– Ralph Waldo Emerson

"Every action has an ancestor of a thought."
– Ralph Waldo Emerson

"That which dominates our imaginations and our thoughts will determine our lives, and our character."
– Ralph Waldo Emerson

"Nature is an endless combination and repetition of a very few laws."
– Ralph Waldo Emerson

"What you do speaks so loudly that no one will ever hear a word you are saying."
– Ralph Waldo Emerson

"A good indignation brings out all one's powers."
– Ralph Waldo Emerson

"It is one of the most beautiful compensations of this life that no one can sincerely try to help another without helping himself."
– Ralph Waldo Emerson

"Happiness is a perfume you cannot pour on others without getting a few drops on yourself."
– Ralph Waldo Emerson

"Judge of your natural character by what you do in your dreams."
– Ralph Waldo Emerson

"To appreciate beauty; to give of one's self, to leave the world a bit better, whether by a healthy child, a garden patch or a redeemed social condition; to have played and laughed with enthusiasm and sung with exultation; to know even one life has breathed easier because you have lived — that is to have succeeded."
– Ralph Waldo Emerson

"There are no days in life so memorable as those which vibrated to some stroke of the imagination."
– Ralph Waldo Emerson

"We are always getting ready to live, but never living."
– Ralph Waldo Emerson

"None of us will ever accomplish anything excellent or commanding except when he listens to this whisper which is heard by him alone."
– Ralph Waldo Emerson

"Life consists of what man is thinking about all day."
– Ralph Waldo Emerson

"The nature of God is a circle of which the center is everywhere and the circumference is nowhere."
– Empedocles

"Why are women immobile? Because so many feel they're waiting for someone to say, 'You're good, you're pretty, I give you permission.'"
– Eve Ensler

"The essence of philosophy is that a man should so live that his happiness shall depend as little as possible on external things."
– Epictetus

"Only the educated are free."
– Epictetus

"First say to yourself what you would be; and then do what you have to do."
– Epictetus

"You are not an isolated unit, but a unique and integral part of the Universe."
– Epictetus

"Skillful pilots gain their reputation from storms and tempest."
– Epicurus

"The summit of happiness is reached when a person is ready to be what he is."
– Desiderius Erasmus

"You and I possess within ourselves, at every moment of our lives, under all circumstances, the power to transform the quality of our lives."
– Werner Erhard

"In youth we learn; in age we understand."
– Marie von Ebner Eshchenbach

"No one can confidently say that he will still be living tomorrow."
– Euridides

"Don't let life discourage you; everyone who got where he is had to begin where he was."
– R. L. Evans

"If you could only sense how important you are to the lives of those you meet; how important you can be to the people you may never dream of. There is something of yourself that you leave at every meeting with another person."
– Roderick Evans

"To read is to empower. To empower is to write. To write is to influence. To influence is to change. To change is to live."
– Jane Evershed

F

"Learning to understand our dreams is a matter of learning how to understand our heart's language."
– Anne Faraday

"Fate is a lazy man's excuse for avoiding curiosity."
– Brian Farrey

"The past is never dead. It's not even past. All of us labor in webs spun long before we were born, webs of heredity and environment, of desire and consequence, of history and eternity. Haunted by wrong turns and roads not taken, we pursue images perceived as new but whose providence dates to the dim dramas of childhood, which are themselves but ripples of consequence echoing down the generations. The quotidian demands of life distract

from this resonance of images and events, but some of us feel it always."
— William Faulkner

"Always dream and shoot higher than you know you can do. Don't bother just to be better than your contemporaries or predecessors. Try to be better than yourself."
— William Faulkner

"Wealth flows from energy and ideas."
— William Feather

"The pain you cause other people cannot be separated from the pain you incur on yourself in the act."
— Frank Ferrante

"It's all really very simple. You don't have to choose between being kind to yourself and others. It's one and the same."
— Piero Ferrucci

"You can tell by how smart people are by what they laugh at."
— Tina Fey

"The important thing is not being afraid to take a chance. Remember, the greatest failure is to not try. Once you find something you love to do, be the best at doing it."
— Debbi Fields

"Never be bullied into silence. Never allow yourself to be made a victim. Accept no one's definition of your life, but define yourself."
— Harvey Fierstein

"Vitality shows not only in the ability to persist but in the ability to start over."
– F. Scott Fitzgerald

"He conquers who endures."
– Aulus Persius Flaccus

"I wonder how many people don't get the one they want, but end up with the one they're supposed to be with."
– Fannie Flagg

"Do not read, as children do, to amuse yourself, or like the ambitious, for the purpose of instruction. No, read in order to live."
– Gustave Flaubert

"Our ignorance of history causes us to slander our own times."
– Gustave Flaubert

"Be steady and well-ordered in your life so that you can be fierce and original in your work."
– Gustave Flaubert

"The most glorious moments in your life are not the so-called days of success, but rather those days when out of dejection and despair you feel rise in you a challenge to life, and the promise of future accomplishments."
– Gustave Flaubert

"Why didn't I learn to treat everything like it was the last time. My greatest regret was how much I believed in the future."
– Jonathan Safron Foer

"To do more for the world than the world does for you. That is success."
– Henry Ford

"Don't find fault, find a remedy; anybody can complain"
– Henry Ford

"You can't build a reputation on what you are going to do."
– Henry Ford

"Most people spend more time and energy going around problems than in trying to solve them."
– Henry Ford

"I suggest that the only books that influence us are those for which we are ready, and which have gone a little farther down our particular path than we have yet got ourselves."
– E. M. Forster

"Normal is not something to aspire to, it's something to get away from."
– Jodie Foster

"The real causes of all our troubles lie within ourselves. The only enemies we have to overcome are our own fears, doubts, selfishness."
– Emmet Fox

"Forgiveness, another word for letting go, is learned drip by drip, day by day, not as an act of altruism but as a necessary cleaning of the past, a purification of our souls so we can live and function effectively in the now. The soul does not grow into its potential fullness when it

harbors past hurt and turns it over and over. That is the way to grow bitterness, not soul."
— Matthew Fox

"No matter how much money you have, you can lose it."
— Michael J. Fox

"My happiness grows in direct proportion to my acceptance, and in inverse proportion to my expectations."
— Michael J. Fox

"I just wish people would realize that anything's possible, if you try; dreams are made, if people try."
— Terry Fox

"To accomplish great things, we must not only act but also dream, not only plan but also believe."
— Anatole France

"It is no use walking anywhere to preach unless our walking is our preaching."
— St. Francis of Assisi

"Start by doing what's necessary; then do what's possible; and suddenly you are doing the impossible."
— St. Francis of Assisi

"If you have a talent, use it in every which way possible. Don't hoard it. Don't dole it out like a miser. Spend it lavishly, like a millionaire intent on going broke."
— Brenda Francis

"Never lose sight of the fact that all human felicity lies in man's imagination and that he cannot think to attain it unless he heeds all his caprices."
– Donatien Alphonse "Marquis de Sade" François

"In spite of everything I still believe that people are really good at heart. I simply can't build up my hopes on a foundation consisting of confusion, misery and death."
– Anne Frank

"I don't think of all the misery, but of the beauty that still remains."
– Anne Frank

"In the long run, the sharpest weapon of all is a kind and gentle spirit."
– Anne Frank

"Parents can only give good advice or put them on the right paths, but the final forming of a person's character lies in their own hands."
– Anne Frank

"Everything can be taken from a man but one thing: the last of the human freedoms — to choose one's attitude in any given set of circumstances, to choose one's own way."
– Victor Frankl

"Some people die at 25 and aren't buried until 75."
– Benjamin Franklin

"Instead of cursing the darkness, light a candle."
– Benjamin Franklin

"Energy and persistence alter all things."
– Benjamin Franklin

"I was always looking outside myself for strength and confidence, but it comes from within. It is there all the time."
– Anna Freud

"Being entirely honest with oneself is a good exercise."
– Sigmund Freud

"Words and magic were in the beginning one and the same thing, and even today words retain much of their magical power."
– Sigmund Freud

"Thought is action in rehearsal."
– Sigmund Freud

"When we share — that is poetry in the prose of life."
– Sigmund Freud

"What you do is what matters, not what you think or say or plan."
– Jason Fried

"People can only hear you when they are moving toward you, and they are not likely to when your words are pursuing them. Even the choicest words lose their power when they are used to overpower. Attitudes are the real figures of speech."
– Edwin H. Friedman

"You can achieve anything you want in life if you have the courage to dream it, the intelligence to make a realistic plan, and the will to see that plan through to the end."
– Sidney A. Friedman

"Greed is a bottomless pit which exhausts the person in an endless effort to satisfy the need without ever reaching satisfaction."
– Erich Fromm

"Only by having faith in ourselves can we be faithful to others."
– Erich Fromm

"A dream is a microscope through which we look at the hidden occurrences in our soul."
– Erich Fromm

"The greater our awareness of intentions, the greater our freedom to choose."
– Gil Fronsdal

"Long after a deed is done, the trace or momentum of the intention left behind it remains as a seed, conditioning our future happiness or unhappiness."
– Gil Fronsdal

"One concept we often impose on our experience is an assumption of permanence, which can put us at odds with the impermanence of all natural processes."
– Gil Fronsdale

"I always entertain great hopes."
– Robert Frost

"The best way out is always through."
– Robert Frost

"It is later in the dark of life that you see forms, constellations. And it is the constellations that are philosophy."
– Robert Frost

"Don't ever take a fence down until you know why it was put up."
– Robert Frost

"I am not a teacher, but an awakener."
– Robert Frost

"There are two kinds of teachers: the kind that fill you with so much quail shot that you can't move, and the kind that just gives you a little prod behind and you jump to the skies."
– Robert Frost

"Stop feeling sorry for yourself and you will be happy."
– Stephen Fry

"It takes a disciplines person to listen to convictions which are different from their own."
– Dorothy Fuldheim

"Don't worry that children never listen to you; worry that they are always watching you."
– Robert Fulghum

"If you have knowledge, let others light their candles in it."
– Margaret Fuller

"Don't be afraid to take a big step when one is indicated. You can't cross a chasm in two small jumps."
– Richard Buckminster Fuller

"In order to change an existing paradigm you do not struggle to try and change the problematic model. You create a new model and make the old one obsolete."
– Richard Buckminster Fuller

"Everything you've learned in school as 'obvious' becomes less and less obvious as you begin to study the universe. For example, there are no solids in the universe. There's not even a suggestion of a solid. There are no absolute continuums. There are no surfaces. There are no straight lines."
– Richard Buckminster Fuller

"In fair weather, prepare for foul."
– Thomas Fuller

"A stumble may prevent a fall."
– Thomas Fuller

G

"If you dare nothing, then when the day is over, nothing is all you will have gained."
– Neil Gaiman

"Fairy tales are more than true: not because they tell us that dragons exist, but because they tell us that dragons can be beaten."
– Neil Gaiman

"No richness is innocent. Richness around the world is the result of other people's poverty."
– Eduardo Galeano

"All truths are easy to understand, once they are discovered; the point is to discover them."
– Galileo Galilei

"Don't you wish there were a knob on the TV to turn up the intelligence? There's one marked 'brightness,' but it doesn't work."
– Leo Anthony Gallagher

"Life is the sum of what you focus on."
– Winifred Gallagher

"The single largest pool of untapped resource in this world is human good intentions that never translate into action."
– Cindy Gallop

"There is force in the universe, which, if we permit it, will flow through us and produce miraculous results."
– Mahatma Gandhi

"Keep your thoughts positive because your thoughts become your words.

Keep your words positive because your words become your behaviors.

Keep your behaviors positive because your behaviors become your habits.

Keep your habits positive because your habits become your values.

Keep your values positive because your values become your destiny."
– Mahatma Gandhi

"An eye for eye only ends up making the whole world blind."
– Mahatma Gandhi

"The difference between what we do and what we are capable of doing would suffice to solve most of the world's problems."
– Mahatma Gandhi

"It is health that is the real wealth and not pieces of gold and silver."
– Mahatma Gandhi

"My life is my teaching."
– Mahatma Gandhi

"An eye for eye only ends up making the whole world blind."
– Mahatma Gandhi

"The future depends on what we do in the present."
– Mahatma Gandhi

"The weak can never forgive. Forgiveness is the attribute of the strong."
– Mahatma Gandhi

"The greatness of a nation and its moral progress can be judged by the way its animals are treated."
– Mahatma Gandhi

"Let us become the change we seek in this world."
– Mahatma Gandhi

"Champions are made from something they have deep inside of them-a desire, a dream, a vision."
– Mahatma Gandhi

"The fragrance always remains on the hand that gives the rose."
– Mahatma Gandhi

"An ounce of practice is worth more than tons of preaching."
– Mahatma Gandhi

"The future depends on what we do in the present."
– Mahatma Gandhi

"The outward freedom that we shall attain will only be in exact proportion to the inward freedom to which we may have grown at a given moment. And if this is a correct view of freedom, our chief energy must be concentrated on achieving reform from within."
– Mahatma Gandhi

"If we are to have real peace, we must begin with the children."
– Mahatma Gandhi

"A small body of determined spirits fired by an unquenchable faith in their mission can alter the course of history."
– Mahatma Gandhi

"As human beings, our greatness lies not so much in being able to remake the world - that is the myth of the atomic age - as in being able to remake ourselves."
– Mahatma Gandhi

"The creative individual has the capacity to free himself from the web of social pressures in which the rest of us are caught. He is capable of questioning the assumptions that the rest of us accept."
– John W. Gardener

"I am I plus my surroundings and if I do not preserve the latter, I do not preserve myself."
– Jose Ortega Y Gasset

"I shut my eyes in order to see."
– Paul Gaugin

"When I'm trusting and being myself, everything in my life reflects this by falling into place easily, often miraculously."
– Shakti Gawain

"Don't you know how sweet and wonderful life can be?"
– Marvin Gaye

"Anybody who thinks money will make you happy, hasn't got money."
– David Geffen

"Be who you are and say what you feel because those who mind don't matter and those who matter don't mind."
– Theodore Geisel

"I like nonsense, it wakes up the brain cells. Fantasy is a necessary ingredient in living, It's a way of looking at life through the wrong end of a telescope. Which is what I do, and that enables you to laugh at life's realities."
– Theodor Seuss Geisel

"The best way to inspire people to superior performance is to convince them by everything you do and by your everyday attitude that you are wholeheartedly supporting them."
– Harold S. Geneen

"When you take charge of your life, there is no longer need to ask permission of other people or society at large. When you ask permission, you give someone veto power over your life."
– Albert F. Geoffrey

"Your impact on the lives of others – your family, the people at your church, your workmates – is cultivated with each decision you make, no matter how small."
– Jim George

"It doesn't matter who you are, or where you come from, or how much money you've got in your pocket. You have your own destiny and your own life ahead of you."
– Stefani Joanne Angelina "Lady Gaga" Germanotta

"Your children are not your children. They are the sons and daughters of Life's longing for itself...
You may house their bodies but not their souls, for their souls dwell in the house of tomorrow, which you cannot visit, not even in your dreams."
– Khalil Gibran

"Music is the language of the spirit. It opens the secret of life bringing peace, abolishing strife."
– Kahlil Gibran

"When you reach the heart of life, you shall find beauty in all things."
– Kahlil Gibran

"Life without love is like a tree without blossom and fruit."
– Kahlil Gibran

"Just because you refuse to acknowledge something, refuse to look at it or think about it, doesn't mean it's not there, that it doesn't affect you and the choices you make in your life."
– Rachel Gibson

"Man cannot discover new oceans unless he has the courage to lose sight of the shore."
– Andre Gide

"You are, after all, what you think. Your emotions are the slaves to your thoughts, and you are the slave to your emotions."
– Elizabeth Gilbert

"You may have tangible wealth untold; Caskets of jewels and coffers of gold. Richer than I you can never be — I had a mother who read to me."
– Strickland Gillilan

"The term 'power' comes from the Latin posse: to do, to be able, to change, to influence or effect. To have power is to possess the capacity to control or direct change. All forms of leadership must make use of power. The central issue of power in leadership is not will it be used? But rather will it be used wisely and well?"
– Al Gini

"Everything is holy! Everybody is holy! Everywhere is holy! Everyday is eternity! Everyman's an angel!"
– Allen Ginsberg

"There are some truths about life that can be expressed only as stories, or songs, or images. Art delights, instructs, consoles. It educates our emotions."
– Dana Gioia

"We love because it's the only true adventure."
– Nikki Giovanni

"If someone listens, or stretches out a hand, or whispers a kind word of encouragement, or attempts to understand a lonely person, extraordinary things begin to happen."
– Loretta Girzatlis

"When something happens to you that is beyond words, life is happening to you. When the Ultimate is happening to you, you are beyond words."
– Swami Dhyan Giten

"To attain to enlightenment is to attain to all. When you are not, you become the whole."
– Swami Dhyan Giten

"Practice isn't the thing you do once you're good. It's the thing you do that makes you good."
– Malcolm Gladwell

"The fewer the facts, the stronger the opinion."
– Arnold H. Glasow

"Success isn't a result of spontaneous combustion. You must set yourself on fire."
– Arnold H. Glasow

"Gossip is just a tool to distract people who have nothing better to do from feeling jealous of those few of us still remaining with noble hearts."
– Anna Godbersen

"The quality of expectations determines the quality of our action."
– Andre Godin

"Instead of wondering when your next vacation is, maybe you should set up a life you don't need to escape from."

– Seth Godin

"At the moment of commitment the entire universe conspires to assist you."

– Johann Wolfgang von Goethe

"What sort of God would it be who only pushed from without?"

– Johann Wolfgang von Goethe

"It seems to never occur to fools that merit and good fortune are closely united."

– Johann Wolfgang von Goethe

"Behavior is a mirror in which every one displays his own image."

– Johann Wolfgang von Goethe

"So divinely is the world organized that every one of us, in our place and time, is in balance with everything else."

– Johann Wolfgang von Goethe

"Nine requisites for contented living: Health enough to make work a pleasure. Wealth enough to support your needs. Strength to battle with difficulties and overcome them. Grace enough to confess your sins and forsake them. Patience enough to toil until some good is accomplished. Charity enough to see some good in your neighbor. Love enough to move you to be useful and helpful to others. Faith enough to make real the things of God. Hope enough to remove all anxious fears concerning the future."

– Johann Wolfgang von Goethe

"Character is formed in the stormy billows of the world."
– Johann Wolfgang von Goethe

"It is in self-limitation that a master first shows himself."
– Johann Wolfgang von Goethe

"Character is formed in the stormy billows of the world."
– Johann Wolfgang von Goethe

"Concerning all acts of initiative and creation, there is one elementary truth, the ignorance of which kills countless ideas and splendid plans: That the moment one definitely commits oneself, the Providence moves too. Whatever you can do or dream you can do, begin it. Boldness has genius, power, and magic in it. Begin it now."
– Johann Wolfgang von Goethe

"Beauty is everywhere a welcome guest."
– Johann Wolfgang von Goethe

"The world is so empty if one thinks only of mountains, rivers & cities; but to know someone who thinks & feels with us, & who, though distant, is close to us in spirit, this makes the earth for us an inhabited garden."
– Johann Wolfgang von Goethe

"Kindness is the golden chain by which society is bound together."
– Johann Wolfgang von Goethe

"Take care of your body with steadfast fidelity. The soul must see through these eyes alone, and if they are dim, the whole world is clouded."
– Johann Wolfgang von Goethe

"Know thyself? If I knew myself, I'd run away."
– Johann Wolfgang von Goethe

"Our task is to say holy yes to the real things of our life."
– Natalie Goldberg

"Of course, a sign doesn't mean anything unless you know how to interpret it."
– Arthur Golden

"Even the most deeply implanted habits of the heart learned in childhood can be reshaped. Emotional learning is lifelong."
– Daniel Goleman

"To exist in this vast universe for a speck of time is the great gift of life. Our tiny sliver of time is our gift of life. It is our only life. The universe will go on, indifferent to our brief existence, but while we are here we touch not just part of that vastness, but also the lives around us. Life is the gift each of us has been given. Each life is our own and no one else's. It is precious beyond all counting. It is the greatest value we can have. Cherish it for what it truly is. Your life is yours alone. Rise up and live it."
– Terry Goodkind

"Never give up. It's like breathing – once you quit, your flame dies letting total darkness extinguish every last gasp of hope. You can't do that. You must continue taking in even the shallowest of breaths, continue putting

forth even the smallest of efforts to sustain your dreams. Don't ever, ever, ever give up."
– Richelle E. Goodrich

"If you really want to get something done, start on it, keep at it, and it will eventually happen."
– Richard H. Goodwin

"It's not that some people have willpower and some don't... It's that some people are ready to change and others are not."
– James Gordon

"The body is a sacred garment. It's your first and last garment; it is what you enter life in and what you depart life with, and it should be treated with honor."
– Martha Graham

"Nothing is more revealing than movement. Actions do speak."
– Martha Graham

"There is a vitality, a life force, an energy, a quickening that is translated through you into action, and because there is only one of you in all of time, this expression is unique. And if you block it, it will never exist through any other medium and it will be lost. The world will not have it. It is not your business to determine how good it is nor how valuable nor how it compares with other expressions. It is your business to keep it yours clearly and directly, to keep the channel open."
– Martha Graham

"Put your good where it will do the most."
– Wavy Gravy

"Winners have simply formed the habit of doing things losers don't like to do."
– Albert Gray

"Everyone is lonely, we have to remember that life is to be lived one day at a time. You cannot worry about the past or future. Happiness is in the now."
– Claudia Gray

"Adventure is not outside, it is within."
– David Grayson

"Imagining the future is a kind of nostalgia. (...) You spend your whole life stuck in the labyrinth, thinking about how you'll escape it one day, and how awesome it will be, and imagining that future keeps you going, but you never do it. You just use the future to escape the present."
– John Green

"There comes a time when we realize that our parents cannot save themselves or save us, that everyone who wades through time eventually gets dragged out to sea by the undertow – that, in short, we are all going."
– John Green

"Despair is the price one pays for setting oneself an impossible aim. It is, one is told, the unforgivable sin, but it is a sin the corrupt or evil man never practices. He always has hope. He never reaches the freezing-point of knowing absolute failure. Only the man of goodwill carries always in his heart this capacity for damnation."
– Graham Greene

"Do not accept the roles that society foists on you. Re-create yourself by forging a new identity, one that commands attention and never bores the audience. Be

the master of your own image rather than letting others define if for you. Incorporate dramatic devices into your public gestures and actions – your power will be enhanced and your character will seem larger than life."
– Robert Greene

"I'm not into isms and asms. There isn't a Catholic moon and a Baptist sun. I know that universal God is universal. I feel that the same God-force that is the mother and father of the pope is also the mother and father of the loneliest man on the planet."
– Dick Gregory

"I skate to where the puck is going to be, not where it has been."
– Wayne Gretzky

"You miss 100 percent of the shots you never take."
– Wayne Gretzky

"No matter who we are, no matter what our circumstances, our feelings and emotions are universal. And music has always been a great way to make people aware of that connection. It can help you open up a part of yourself and express feelings you didn't know you were feeling. It's risky to let that happen. But it's a risk you have to take-because only then will you find you're not alone."
– Josh Groban

"The new formula of physics describes humans as paradoxical beings who have two complementary aspects: They can show properties of Newtonian objects and also infinite fields of consciousness."
– Stanislav Grog

H

"Let someone love you just the way you are – as flaws as you might be, as unattractive as you sometimes feel, and as unaccomplished as you think you are. To believe that you must hide all the parts of you that are broken, out of fear that someone else is incapable of loving what is less than perfect, is to believe that sunlight is incapable of entering a broken window and illuminating a dark room."
– Marc Hack

"As a child my family's menu consisted of two choices: take it or leave it."
– Buddy Hackett

"I have learned so much from God that I no longer call myself a Christian, a Hindu, a Muslim, a Buddhist, a Jew. The truth has shared so much of itself with me that I can no longer call myself a man, a woman, an angel, or even pure soul. Love has befriended Hafiz so completely, it has turned to ash and freed me of every concept and image my mind has ever known."
– Hafiz

"If you win, but don't help somebody when you should have, what kind of win is that?"
– Bjoernar Hakensmoen

"Growth is painful. Change is painful. But nothing is as painful as staying stuck somewhere you don't belong."
– Mandy Hale

"Acting on a good idea is better than just having a good idea."
– Robert Half

"It is books that are a key to the wide world; if you can't do anything else, read all that you can."
– Jane Hamilton

"My father had taught me to be nice first, because you can always be mean later, but once you've been mean to someone, they won't believe the nice anymore. So be nice, be nice, until it's time to stop being nice, then destroy them."
– Laurell K. Hamilton

"No name-calling truly bites deep unless, in some dark part of us, we believe it. If we are confident enough then it is just noise."
– Laurell K. Hamilton

"I still have great faith in what is good and right in all of us."
– Marvin Hamlisch

"The essence of nonviolence is love. Out of love and the willingness to act selflessly, strategies, tactics, and techniques for a nonviolent struggle arise naturally. Nonviolence is not a dogma; it is a process."
– Thich Nhat Hanh

"Keeping your body healthy is an expression of gratitude to the whole cosmos, the trees, the clouds, everything."
– Thich Nhat Hanh

"Every day we are engaged in a miracle which we don't even recognize: a blue sky, white clouds, green leaves, the black, curious eyes of a child – our own two eyes. All is a miracle."
– Thich Nhat Hanh

"In Buddhism, we talk of meditation as an act of awkening, to be awake to the fact that the earth is in danger and living species are in danger."
– Thich Nhat Hanh

"People deal too much with the negative, with what is wrong. Why not try and see positive things, to just touch those things and make them bloom?"
– Thich Nhat Hanh

"When another person makes you suffer, it is because he suffers deeply within himself, and his suffering is spilling over. He does not need punishment; he needs help."
– Thich Naht Hanh

"We have more possibilities available in each moment than we realize."
– Thich Nhat Hanh

"To make real friends you have to put yourself out there. Sometimes people will let you down, but you can't let that stop you. If you get hurt, you just pick yourself up, dust off your feelings, and try again."
– Kristin Hannah

"People inspire you or they drain you. Pick them wisely."
– Hans F. Hansen

"Taking in the good is not about putting a happy shiny face on everything, nor is it about turning away from the hard things in life. It's about nourishing inner well-being, contentment, and peace – refuges to which you can always return."
– Rick Hanson

"What man knows is little enough and most of his general concepts in every field are vitiated by the artificial concepts he has created to cover his ignorance. These concepts must be destroyed. One tool exists that can accomplish this destruction, and this tool is in your hands. It is simply curiosity – the instinct to ask and to question. It should be kept sharp and used without mercy."
– Charles Hapgood

"A positive attitude is perhaps more important at home than anywhere else. As spouses and parents, one of our most vital roles is to help those we love feel good about themselves."
– Keith Harrell

"Regret for the things we did can be tempered by time; it is regret for the things we did not do that is inconsolable."
– Sidney J. Harris

"Life is difficult for everyone. We all have stress and we all need someone in our lives that we can lean on. Never think that you cannot talk to someone because they have problems to or that your friend or loved one would be better off without you or your problems. You'll soon find out that they need you just as much as you need them."
– Joshua Hartzell

"By acknowledging your own fears and insecurities and corruptions, you start to have a much more gentle and profound sense of where they come from in other people."
– Andrew Harvey

"Vision isn't enough unless combined with venture. It's not enough to stare up the steps unless we also step up the stairs."
– Vance Havner

"You may be whatever you resolve to be. Determine to be something in the world, and you will be something. 'I cannot,' never accomplished anything; 'I will try,' has wrought wonders."
– J. Hawes

"When you're a kid, everyone, all the world, encourages you to follow your dreams. But when you're older, somehow they act offended if you even try."
– Ethan Hawke

"The most unrealistic person in the world is the cynic, not the dreamer. Hopefulness only makes sense when it doesn't make sense to be hopeful. This is your century. Take it and run as if your life depends on it."
– Paul Hawken

"In each of you are one quadrillion cells, 90 percent of which are not human cells. Your body is a community, and without those other microorganisms you would perish in hours. Each human cell has 400 billion molecules conducting millions of processes between trillions of atoms. The total cellular activity in one human body is staggering: one septillion actions at any one moment, a one with twenty-four zeros after it. In a millisecond, our body has undergone ten times more processes than there are stars in the universe — exactly what Charles Darwin foretold when he said science would discover that each living creature was a 'little universe, formed of a host of self-propagating organisms, inconceivably minute and as numerous as the stars of heaven.'"
– Paul Hawken

"The greatest enemy of knowledge is not ignorance, it is the illusion of knowledge."
– Stephen Hawking

"All of us must cross the line between ignorance and insight many times before we truly understand."
– David Hawkins

"Happiness is like a butterfly which, when pursued, is always beyond our grasp, but, if you will sit down quietly, may alight upon you."
– Nathaniel Hawthorne

"It's extremely important that you love and appreciate who you are. Too many of us have grown up believing that we're really not good enough, or were not worthy, or we don't deserve. We are divine, magnificent expressions of life and we have to know that and experience it and rejoice in it."
– Louise Hay

"The story of a love is not important — what is important is that one is capable of love. It is perhaps the only glimpse we are permitted of eternity."
– Helen Hayes

"From your parents you learn love and laughter and how to put one foot before the other. But when books are opened you discover that you have wings."
– Helen Hayes

"In terms of being late or not starting at all, then it's never too late."
– Alison Headley

"Underneath all the twists and turns of relationships, love is the only and ultimate truth between souls."
– Kathy Hearn

"People change and forget to tell each other."
– Lillian Hellman

"As long as you have life and breath, believe. Believe for those who cannot. Believe even if you have stopped believing. Believe for the sake of the dead, for love, to keep your heart beating, believe. Never give up, never despair, let no mystery confound you into the conclusion that mystery cannot be yours."
– Mark Helprin

"The best people possess a feeling for beauty, the courage to take risks, the discipline to tell the truth, the capacity for sacrifice. Ironically, their virtues make them vulnerable; they are often wounded, sometimes destroyed."
– Ernest Hemmingway

"Music is my religion."
– Jimi Hendrix

"I've been lucky. Opportunities don't often come along. So, when they do, you have to grab them."
– Audrey Hepburn

"I believe in pink. I believe that laughing is the best calorie burner. I believe in kissing, kissing a lot. I believe in being strong when everything seems to be going wrong. I believe that happy girls are the prettiest girls. I believe that tomorrow is another day and I believe in miracles."
– Audrey Hepburn

"The best thing to hold onto in life is each other."
– Audrey Hepburn

"The soul is dyed the color of its thoughts. Think only on those things that are in line with your principles and can bear the full light of day. The content of your character is your choice. Day by day, what you think, and what you do is who you become. Your integrity is your destiny. It is the light that guides your way."
– Heraclitus

"A lean compromise is better than a fat lawsuit."
– George Herbert

"Sometimes life holds more than people allow themselves to see. Such individuals may continue to live as though they are blind for eternities before realizing they were merely clamping their eyes shut."
– Emily Herr

"Fundamentally the marksman aims at himself."
– Eugen Herrigel

"When I was young, I used to admire intelligent people; as I grow older, I admire kind people."
– Abraham Joshua Heschel

"Self-respect is the root of discipline: The sense of dignity grows with the ability to say no to oneself."
– Abraham Joshua Heschel

"I have always believed, and I still believe, that whatever good or bad fortune may come our way we can always give it meaning and transform it into something of value."
– Hermann Hesse

"Some people regard themselves as perfect, but only because they demand little of themselves."
– Hermann Hesse

"Every man is more than just himself; he also represents the unique, the very special and always significant and remarkable point at which the world's phenomena intersect, only once in this way, and never again. That is why every man's story is important, eternal, sacred; that is why every man, as long as he lives and fulfills the will of nature, is wondrous, and worthy of consideration. In each individual the spirit has become

flesh, in each man the creation suffers, within each one a redeemer is nailed to the cross."
– Hermann Hesse

"Loneliness is the way by which destiny endeavors to lead man to himself."
– Hermann Hesse

"Every man is more than just himself; he also represents the unique, the very special and always significant and remarkable point at which the world's phenomena intersect, only once in this way, and never again."
– Hermann Hesse

"I gave myself permission to care, because there are a lot of people in this world who are afraid of caring, who are afraid of showing they care because it's uncool. It's uncool to have passion. It's so much easier to lose when you've shown everyone how much you don't care if you win or lose. It's much harder to lose when you show that you care, but you'll never win unless you also stand to lose. I've said it before. Don't be afraid of your passion, give it free reign, and be honest and work hard and it will all turn out just fine."
– Tom Hiddleston

"Strong lives are motivated by dynamic purposes."
– Kenneth Hildebrand

"Men take on the nature, the habits, and the power of thought of those with whom they associate."
– Napoleon Hill

"Cherish your visions and your dreams, as they are the children of your soul, the blueprints of your ultimate achievements."
– Napoleon Hill

"Every adversity, every failure, every heartache carries with it the seed of an equal or greater benefit."
– Napolean Hill

"If you can't do great things, do small things in a great way."
– Napoleon Hill

"If I am not for myself, who is for me? And if I am only for myself, what am I? And if not now, when?"
– Hillel

"No one has ever made himself great by showing how small someone else is."
– Irvin Himmel

"Forget yourself and go to work."
– Bryant S. Hinckley

"True love is not so much a matter of romance as it is a matter of anxious concern for the well-being of one's companion."
– Gordon B. Hinckley

"Try a little harder to be a little better."
– Gordon B. Hinckley

"Our lives are, in reality, the sum total of our seemingly unimportant decisions and of our capacity to live by those decisions."
– Gordon B. Hinckley

"The trick is to enjoy life. Don't wish away your days, waiting for better ones ahead."
– Marjorie Pay Hinckley

"I know it is hard for you young mothers to believe that almost before you can turn around the children will be gone and you will be alone with your husband. You had better be sure you are developing the kind of love and friendship that will be delightful and enduring. Let the children learn from your attitude that he is important. Encourage him. Be kind. It is a rough world, and he, like everyone else, is fighting to survive. Be cheerful. Don't be a whiner."
– Marjorie Pay Hinckley

"Extreme measures are very appropriate for extreme disease."
– Hippocrates

"The world I am trying to understand is one in which men think they want one thing and then upon getting it, find out to their dismay that they don't want it nearly as much as they thought or don't want it at all and that something else, of which they were hardly aware, is what they really want."
– Albert Hirschman

"We never know the quality of someone else's life, though we seldom resist the temptation to assume and pass judgement."
– Tami Hoag

"The problem is never how to get new, innovative thoughts into your mind, but how to get old ones out. Every mind is a building filled with archaic furniture.

Clean out a corner of your mind and creativity will instantly fill it."
– Dee Hock

"We grow small trying to be great."
– David Hockney

"Some blind faithfully; some see."
– T.F. Hodge

"It doesn't matter what we are. It matters what we do."
– Michelle Hodkin

"Do you really want to be happy? You can begin by being appreciative of who you are and what you've got."
– Benjamin Hoff

"The capacity for getting along with our neighbor depends to a large extent on the capacity for getting along with ourselves. The self-respecting individual will try to be as tolerant of his neighbor's shortcomings as he is of his own."
– Eric Hoffer

"Rudeness is a weak man's imitation of strength."
– Eric Hoffer

"Self righteousness is a loud din raised to drown the voice of guilt within us."
– Eric Hoffer

"The ability to simplify means to eliminate the unnecessary so that the necessary may speak."
– Hans Hofmann

"There is absolutely nothing that separates the elite from the paupers except their expectations. If you wish

to rise above the masses, then let the fire burn fiercely within you. Do this, and it shall be done!"
– J. Arthur Holcombe

"Humanity and divinity will be identical when we recognize divinity in humanity."
– Ernest Holmes

"A moments insight is sometimes worth a life's experience."
– Oliver Wendell Holmes

"One's mind, once stretched by a new idea, never regains its original dimensions."
– Oliver Wendell Holmes

"The best of a book is not the thought which it contains, but the thought which it suggests; just as the charm of music dwells not in the tones but in the echoes of our hearts."
– Oliver Wendell Holmes

"The best of a book is not the thought which it contains, but the thought which it suggests; just as the charm of music dwells not in the tones but in the echoes of our hearts."
– Oliver Wendell Holmes

"Life is painting a picture, not doing a sum."
– Oliver Wendell Holmes, Jr.

"Never regret. If it's good, it's wonderful. If it's bad, it's experience."
– Victoria Holt

"By mutual confidence and mutual aid – great deeds are done, and great discoveries made."
– Homer

"Yet, taught by time, my heart has learned to glow for other's good, and melt at other's woe."
– Homer

"Taking no chances means wasting your dreams."
– Ellen Hopkins

"The world is charged with the grandeur of God."
– Gerard Manley Hopkins

"Remember when life's path is steep to keep your mind even."
– Horace

"The envious man grows lean at the success of his neighbor."
– Horace

"It's not the load that breaks you down, it's how you carry it."
– Lena Horne

"All live is sacred. We come into life as sacred beings. When we abuse the sacredness of life, we affect all creation."
– Chief Arvol Looking Horse

"I want you to learn the lesson of the lotus. This flower springs forth from muddy waters. It raises its delicate petals to the sun and perfumes the world while, at the same time, its roots cling to the elemental muck,

the very essence of the mortal experience. Without that soil, the flower would wither and die."
– Colleen Houck

"You must learn to take a step back and visualize the whole piece. If you focus only on the thread given to you, you lose sight of what it can become. "
– Colleen Houck

"Don't allow yourself to become disheartened when the thread doesn't suit or seems unsightly to you. Wait and watch. Be patient and devoted. As the threads twist and turn, you will begin to understand, and you will see the pattern finally materialize in all its splendor."
– Colleen Houck

"To have regret is to be disappointed with yourself and your choices. Those who are wise, see their life like stepping stones across a great river. Everyone misses a stone from time to time. No one can cross the river without getting wet. Success is measured by your arrival on the other side, not on how muddy your shoes are. Regrets are only felt by those who do not understand life's purpose. They become so disillusioned that they stand still in the river and do not take the next leap."
– Colleen Houck

"If you want your life to be a magnificent story, then begin by realizing that you are the author and everyday you have the opportunity to write a new page."
– Mark Houlahan

"Indeed, this need of individuals to be right is so great that they are willing to sacrifice themselves, their relationships, and even love for it."
– Reuel Howe

"I would rather be able to appreciate things I cannot have than to have things I am not able to appreciate."
– Elbert Hubbard

"There is no failure except in no longer trying."
– Ebert Hubbard

"There is no defeat except from within, no really insurmountable barrier save our own inherent weakness of purpose."
– Elbert Hubbard

"We are weaving character every day, and the way to weave the best character is to be kind and to be useful. Think right, act right; it is what we think and do that makes us who we are."
– Elbert Hubbard

"Yes, I am me, but what animates me is what animates Uncle Bob, the cat, the tree, the rock, and all that is. We are packaged differently, but we share the same essence. There are many of us and we are not the same but we are all one."
– Cheri Huber

"Like a welcome summer rain, humor may suddenly cleanse and cool the earth, the air, and you."
– Langston Hughes

"Those who do not weep, do not see."
– Victor Hugo

"Have courage for the great sorrows of life and patience for the small ones; and when you have laboriously accomplished your daily task, go to sleep in peace. God is awake."
– Victor Hugo

"Certain thoughts are prayers. There are moments when, whatever be the attitude of the body, the soul is on its knees."
– Victor Hugo

"Oh, my friend, it's not what they take away from you that counts. It's what you do with what you have left."
– Hubert Humphrey

"The greatest healing therapy is friendship and love."
– Hubert Humphrey

"I have the nerve to walk my own way, however hard, in my search for reality, rather than climb upon the rattling wagon of wishful illusions."
– Zora Neale Hurston

"Some people could look at a mud puddle and see an ocean with ships."
– Zora Neale Hurston

"If you talked to your friends the way you talk to your body, you'd have no friends left at all."
– Marcia Hutchinson

"It is a bit embarrassing to have been concerned with the human problem all one's life and find at the end that one has no more to offer by way of advice than 'Try to be a little kinder.'"
– Aldous Huxley

"Cynical realism is the intelligent man's best excuse for doing nothing in an intolerable situation."
– Aldous Huxley

"Every man's memory is his private literature."
– Aldous Huxley

"There will be in the next generation or so a pharmacological method of making people love their servitude and productin dictatorship without tears so to speak. Producting a kidn of painless concentration camp for entire socieities so that people will in fact have their liberties taken away from them, but will rather enjoy it, because they will be distracted from any desire to rebel by propaganda, or brainwashing, or brainwashing enhanced by pharmacological methods. And this seems to be the final revolution."
– Aldous Huxley

"Happiness is not achieved by the conscious pursuit of happiness; it is generally the by-product of other activities."
– Aldous Huxley

"I wanted to change the world. But I have found that the only thing one can be sure of changing is oneself."
– Aldous Huxley

"That's the way to tell a true story from a made-up one. A made-up story always has a neat and tidy end. But true stories don't end, at least until their heroes and heroines die, and not then really because the things they did and didn't do, sometimes live on."
– Elspeth Huxley

"Sit down before fact as a little child, be prepared to give up every preconceived notion, follow humbly wherever and to whatever abysses nature leads, or you shall learn nothing. I have only begun to learn content

and peace of mind since I have resolved at all risks to do this."
– Thomas Henry Huxley

I

"A thousand words leave not the same deep impression as does a single deed."
– Henrik Ibsen

"A great revolution in just one single individual will help achieve a change in the destiny of a society and, further, will enable a change in the destiny of humankind."
– Daisaku Ikeda

"It is impossible to build one's own happiness on the unhappiness of others. This perspective is at the heart of Buddhist teachings."
– Daisaku Ikeda

"Life is painful. It has thorns, like the stem of a rose. Culture and art are the roses that bloom on the stem. The flower is yourself, your humanity. Art is the liberation of the humanity inside yourself."
– Daisaku Ikeda

"A great human revolution in just a single individual will help achieve a change in the destiny of a nation and, further, can even enable a change in the destiny of all humankind."
– Daisaku Ikeda

"The time to be happy is now. The place to be happy is here. The way to be happy is to make others so."
– Robert Green Ingersoll

"If you are seeking creative ideas, go out walking. Angels whisper to a man when he goes for a walk."
– Raymond Inmon

"Some of the most significant problems of humankind can only be fundamentally approached as matters of conscience, commitments of the human spirit, and endeavors of whole communities, local and global."
– Thomas S. Inui

"Who can tell what miracles love has in store for us if only we can find the courage to become with it? Everything we now know is only a beginning of another knowing that has no end."
– Iqbal

"To act as soil and sustenance for another person's spirit is both a privilege and a responsibility. Never take it lightly."
– Toby Israel

"The final destination of a journey is not, after all, the last item on the agenda, but rather some understanding, however simple or provisional, of what one has seen."
– Pico Iyer

J

"Your children need your presence more than your presents."
– Jesse Jackson

"It's no accident that things are more likely to go your way when you stop worrying about whether you're going to win or lose, and focus your full attention on what is happening right this moment."
– Phil Jackson

"My mother has always been unhappy with what I do. She would much rather I do something nice, like be a bricklayer.
– Mick Jagger

"Be not afraid of life. Believe that life is worth living, and your belief will help create the fact."
– Henry James

"Live all you can: it's a mistake not to. It doesn't matter what you do in particular, so long as you have had your life. If you haven't had that, what have you had?"
– Henry James

"I don't want everyone to like me; I should think less of myself if some people did."
– Henry James

"Obstacles are those frightening things you see when you take you eyes off your goal."
– Henry James

"Do your own thing on your own terms and get what you came here for."
– Oliver James

"Our lives are like islands in the sea, or like trees in the forest, which co-mingle their roots in the darkness underground."
– William James

"The greatest revolution of our generation is the discovery that human beings, by changing the inner attitudes of their minds, can change the outer aspects of their lives."
– William James

"For him who confesses, shams are over and realities have begun; he has exteriorized his rottenness. If he has not actually got rid of it, he at least no longer smears it over with a hypocritical show of virtue."
– William James

"Most people never run far enough on their first wind to find out they've got a second. Give your dreams all you've got and you'll be amazed at the energy that comes out of you."
– William James

"Nothing is so fatiguing as the eternal hanging on of an uncompleted task."
– William James

"It is as important to cultivate your silent power as it is your word power."
– William James

"Be not afraid of life. Believe that life is worth living, and your belief will help create the fact."
– William James

"We are like islands in the seas, separate on the surface, but connected in the deep."
– William James

"Most people live, whether physically, intellectually or morally, in a very restricted circle of their potential being. They make very small use of their possible consciousness, and of their soul's resources in general, much like a man who, out of his whole bodily organism, should get into a habit of using and moving only his little finger."
– William James

"Act as if what you do makes a difference. It does."
– William James

"The motive behind criticism often determines its validity. Those who care criticize where necessary. Those who envy criticize the moment they think that they have found a weak spot."
– Criss Jami

"Spending time looking for what is missing in your life is futile; if you fail to look within yourself. When we challenge everything we believe we are, we reveal that which we never knew about our own selves."
– Nicolas G. Janovsky

"The best epiphanies approach their revelations indirectly, through imagery, metaphor, and symbol rather than through direct statement. In short, they arrive with some elusiveness, like insight itself."
– David Jauss

"I find that the harder I work, the more luck I seem to have."
– Thomas Jefferson

"I do not believe in taking the right decision, I take a decision and make it right."
– Muhammad Ali Jinnah

"Your time is limited, so don't waste it living someone else's life."
– Steve Jobs

"The only way to do great work is to love what you do. If you haven't found it yet, keep looking. Don't settle. As with all matters of the heart, you'll know when you find it."
– Steve Jobs

"When you are in a state of nonacceptance, it's difficult to learn. A clenched fist cannot receive a gift, and a clenched psyche — grasped tightly against the reality of what must not be accepted – cannot easily receive a lesson."
– Roger John

"To be in your children's memories tomorrow, You have to be in their lives today."
– Barbara Johnson

"Appreciate your learning process, for it is of equal value to have realized there is a need for change as for the change itself."
– Beth Johnson

"I have a personal philosophy in life: kindness begets kindness."
– Drew Johnson

"When you walk up to opportunity's door, don't knock it, kick that bitch in, smile, and introduce yourself."
– Dwayne Johnson

"Hope is itself a species of happiness, and, perhaps, the chief happiness which this world affords."
– Samuel Johnson

"Patriotism is the last refuge of the scoundrel."
– Samuel Johnson

"Example is always more efficacious than precept."
– Samuel Johnson

"Integrity is telling myself the truth."
– Spencer Johnson

"We can be drones addicted to crap, destruction, and material possessions we gather to impress upon people we don't even really like, or we can make our life count for something real and meaningful and make it count that we graced the planet at all.

Life is either a dance to remember or a dance to forget. Let's make it one to remember. Let's make it elegant, honorable, and saturated with truth."

– Harley "Durianrider" Johnstone

"I try to tell the young kids there are two cardinal rules: You should approach creativity with humility and have your success with grace. It's a gift from God. You don't deserve it. You are a vehicle of a higher power. Don't abuse it."

– Quincy Jones

"If you don't risk anything – you're risking even more."

– Erica Jong

"Don't compromise yourself. You are all you've got."

– Janis Joplin

"I've missed more than 9,000 shots in my career. I've lost almost 300 games. 26 times, I've been trusted to take the game winning shot and missed. I've failed over and over and over again in my life. And that is why I succeed."

– Michael Jordan

"Obstacles don't have to stop you. If you run into a wall, don't turn around and give up. Figure out how to climb it, go through it, or work around it."

– Michael Jordan

"When a man's self is hidden from everybody else, it seems also to become hidden even from himself, and it permits disease and death to gnaw into his substance without his clear knowledge."
– Sidney Jourard

"Be kind, for everyone you meet is fighting a hard battle."
– Philo Judaeus

"The body is the soul's house. Shouldn't we therefore take care of our house so that it doesn't fall into ruin?"
– Philo Judaeus

"Perpetrators are shameless, and they put their shame on their victims."
– Ashley Judd

"Just as the material of the body that is ready for life has need of the psyche in order to be capable of life, so psyche presupposes the living body in order that its images may live."
– Carl Gustav Jung

"The meeting of two personalities is like the contact of two chemical substances. If there is any reaction, both are transformed."
– Carl Gustav Jung

"Even a happy life cannot be without a measure of darkness, and the word happy would lose its meaning if it were not balanced by sadness. It is far better take things as they come along with patience and equanimity."
– Carl Gustav Jung

"Narcissism thus involves a withdrawal of instinctual energy and an investment of libido in the ego. This investment in the ego implies that the person is unable to love or relate with others and is self-absorbed."
– Carl Gustav Jung

"Your vision will become clear only when you look into your heart. Who looks outside, dreams. Who looks inside, awakens."
– Carl Gustav Jung

"That which we do not confront in ourselves we will meet as fate."
– Carl Gustav Jung

"Our intellect has achieved the most tremendous things, but in the meantime our spiritual dwelling has fallen into disrepair."
– Carl Gustav Jung

"The sole purpose of human existence is to kindle a light in the darkness of mere being."
– Carl Gustav Jung

"In psychotherapy, enthusiasm is the secret of success."
– Carl Gustav Jung

"The privilege of a lifetime is to become who you truly are."
– Carl Gustav Jung

"I have frequently seen people become neurotic when they content themselves with inadequate or wrong answers to the questions of life. They seek position, marriage, reputation, outward success of money, and remain unhappy and neurotic even when they have

attained what they were seeking. Such people are usually confined within too narrow a spiritual horizon. Their life has not sufficient content, sufficient meaning. If they are enabled to develop into more spacious personalities, the neurosis generally disappears."
– Carl Gustav Jung

"The debt we owe to the play of imagination is incalculable."
– Carl Gustav Jung

"The world today hangs by a thin thread, and that thread is the psyche of man."
– Carl Gustav Jung

K

"Each difficult moment has the potential to open my eyes and open my heart."
– Myla Kabat-Zinn

"If we cannot see how what we are doing or not doing is contributing to things being the way that they are, then logically we have no basis at all, zero leverage, for changing the way things are – except from the outside, by persuasion or force."
– Adam Kahane

"Don't be disquieted in time of adversity. Be firm with dignity and self-reliant with vigor."
– Chiang Kai-Shek

"We should try to leave the world a better place than when we entered it. As individuals, we can make a difference, whether it is to probe the secrets of Nature, to clean up the environment and work for peace and social justice, or to nurture the inquisitive, vibrant spirit of the young by being a mentor and a guide."
– Michio Kaku

"Dream. Dream. Dream. Dreams transform into thoughts. And thoughts result in action."
– A.P.J Abdul Kalam

"The brain gives the heart its sight. The heart gives the brain its vision."
– Rob Kall

"Do what you love, think what you feel and live the way you want."
– Santosh Kalwar

"The things you do for yourself are gone when you are gone, but the things you do for others remain as your legacy."
– Kalu Ndukwe Kalu

"Find the seed at the bottom of your heart and bring forth a flower."
– Shigenori Kameoka

"Behaviors and thoughts that relate to hope, love, and happiness can change the brain — just as fear, stress, and anxiety can change it."
– Eric Kanel

"Struggling and suffering are the essence of a life worth living. If you're not pushing yourself beyond the comfort zone, if you're not demanding more from

yourself – expanding and learning as you go – you're choosing a numb existence. Youære denying yourself an extraordinary trip."
– Dean Karnazes

"Run when you can, walk if you have to, crawl if you must; just never give up."
– Dean Karnazes

"It takes more courage to reveal insecurities than to hide them, more strength to relate to people than to dominate them, more 'manhood' to abide by thought-out principles rather than blind reflex. Toughness is in the soul and spirit, not in muscles and an immature mind."
– Alex Karras

"The best way to predict the future is to create it."
– Alan Kay

"By believing passionately in something that still does not exist, we create it. The nonexistent is whatever we have not sufficiently desired."
– Nikos Kazantzakis

"We are kept from the experience of spirit because our inner world is cluttered with past traumas. As we begin to clear away this clutter, the energy of divine light and love begins to glow through our beings."
– Tomas Keating

"The poetry of Earth is never dead."
– John Keats

"Failure is, in a sense, the highway to success, inasmuch as every discovery of what is false leads us to seek earnestly after what is true."
– John Keats

"That's what happens when you're angry at people. You make them part of your life."
– Garrison Keillor

"Some luck lies in not getting what you thought you wanted but getting what you have, which once you have it you may be smart enough to see is what you would have wanted had you known."
– Garrison Keillor

"The only thing worse than being blind is having sight but no vision."
– Helen Keller

"There is no king who has not had a slave among his ancestors, and no slave who has not had a king among his."
– Helen Keller

"Although the world is full of suffering, it is also full of overcoming it."
– Helen Keller

"One can never consent to creep when one feels the compulsion to soar."
– Helen Keller

"We need limitations and temptations to open our inner selves, dispel our ignorance, tear off disguises, throw down old idols, and destroy false standards. Only by such rude awakenings can we be led to dwell in a place where we are less cramped, less hindered by the

ever-insistent External. Only then do we discover a new capacity and appreciation of goodness and beauty and truth."
– Helen Keller

"Tell others of the positive effects of their actions. It will help return the kindness to you."
– Dan Kelly

"The poor man is not he who is without a cent, but he who is without a dream."
– Harry Kemp

"Keep the peace within yourself. Then you can also bring peace to others."
– Thomas A. Kempis

"Some people follow their dreams, others hunt them down and beat them mercilessly into submission."
– Neil Kendall

"A lot of disappointed people have been left standing on the street corner waiting for the bus marked perfection."
– Donald Kennedy

"Physical fitness is not only one of the most important keys to a healthy body, it is the basis of dynamic and creative intellectual activity."
– John F. Kennedy

"Each time a person stands up for an ideal, or acts to improve the lot of others, or strikes out against injustice, he sends forth a tiny ripple of hope, and crossing each other from a million different centers of energy and

daring, these ripples build a current that can sweep down the mightiest walls of oppression and resistance."
– Robert F. Kennedy

"Tragedy and adversary are the stones we sharpen our swords against so we can fight new battles."
– Sherrilyn Kenyon

"Sometimes you just need to relax and trust that things will work out. Let go a little and just let life happen."
– Kody Keplinger

"Education is too important to be left solely to the educators."
– Francis Keppel

"In the end, you won't remember the time you spent working in the office or mowing your lawn. Climb that damn mountain!"
– Jack Kerouac

"You can count how many seeds are in the apple, but not how many apples are in the seed."
– Ken Kersey

"Believe in yourself and there will come a day when others will have no choice but to believe with you."
– Cynthia Kersey

"You can't have a better tomorrow if you are thinking about yesterday all the time."
– Charles F. Kettering

"To see your drama clearly is to be liberated from it."
– Ken Keyes

"Very often in everyday life one sees that by losing one's temper with someone who has already lost his, one does not gain anything but only sets out upon the path of stupidity. He who has enough self-control to stand firm at the moment when the other person is in a temper, wins in the end. It is not he who has spoken a hundred words aloud who has won; it is he who has perhaps spoken only one word."
– Hazrat Inayat Khan

"Some people look for a beautiful place. Others make a place beautiful."
– Hazrat Inayat Khan

"Dead yesterdays and unborn tomorrows, why fret about it, if today be sweet."
– Omar Khayyam

"Refuse to allow yourselves to be swept by any fear psychosis or to be stampeded into any attitude through which the anxiety and unrest and distress in the world can overwhelm you. Strive to stand in spiritual being. Each morning, in your meditation, seek to take that attitude with a new and fresh definiteness and to hold it during the hours of service which lie ahead each day."
– Djwhal Khul

"Hope is passion for what is possible"
– Soren Kierkegaard

"Stress is not what happens to us. It's our response to what happens. And response is something we can choose."
– Maureen Kiloran

"Remember, we all stumble, every one of us. That's why it's a comfort to go hand-in-hand."
– Emily Kimbrough

"If you lose hope, somehow you lose the vitality that keeps life moving, you lose that courage to be, that quality that helps you go on in spite of it all. And so today I still have a dream."
– Martin Luther King, Jr.

"All of life is interrelated. We are all caught in an inescapable network of mutuality, tied to a single garment of destiny. Whatever affects one directly affects all indirectly."
– Martin Luther King, Jr.

"Every human being has etched in his personality the indelible stamp of the Creator."
– Martin Luther King, Jr.

"Darkness cannot drive out darkness; only light can do that. Hate cannot drive out hate; only love can do that."
– Martin Luther King, Jr.

"Nonviolence means avoiding not only external physical violence but also internal violence of spirit. You not only refuse to shoot a man, but you refuse to hate him."
– Martin Luther King, Jr.

"The quality, not the longevity, of one's life is what is important."
– Martin Luther King, Jr.

"In the end, we will remember not the words or our enemies, but the silence of our friends."
– Martin Luther King, Jr.

"If you can't fly then run, if you can't run then walk, if you can't walk then crawl, but whatever you do you have to keep moving forward."
– Martin Luther King, Jr.

"One of the great liabilities of history is that all too many people fail to remain awake through great periods of social change. Every society has its protectors of status quo and its fraternities of the indifferent who are notorious for sleeping through revolutions. Today, our very survival depends on our ability to stay awake, to adjust to new ideas, to remain vigilant and to face the challenge of change."
– Martin Luther King, Jr.

"Violence never brings permanent peace. It solves no social problem: it merely creates new and more complicated ones. Violence is impractical because it is a descending spiral ending in destruction for all. It is immoral because it seeks to humiliate the opponent rather than win his understanding: it seeks to annihilate rather than convert. Violence is immoral because it thrives on hatred rather than love. It destroys community and makes brotherhood impossible. It leaves society in monologue rather than dialogue. Violence ends up defeating itself. It creates bitterness in the survivors and brutality in the destroyers."
– Martin Luther King, Jr.

"If you don't have the time to do something right, where are you going to find the time to fix it?"
– Stephen King

"Amateurs sit and wait for inspiration, the rest of us just get up and go to work."
– Stephen King

"The very least you can do in your life is to figure out what you hope for. And the most you can do is live inside that hope. Not admire it from a distance but live right in it, under its roof."
– Barbara Kingsolver

"You have powers you never dreamed of. You can do things you never thought you could do. There are no limitations in what you can do except the limitations of your own mind."
– Darwin P. Kingsley

"If you can't be honest with your friends and colleagues and loved ones, then what is life all about?"
– Sophie Kinsella

"Whether you live to be 50 or 100 makes no difference, if you made no difference in the world."
– Jarod Kintz

"Just because I liked something at one point in time doesn't mean I'll always like it, or that I have to go on liking it at all points in time as an unthinking act of loyalty to who I am as a person, based solely on who I was as a person. To be loyal to myself is to allow myself to grow and change, and challenge who I am and what I think. The only thing I am for sure is unsure, and this means I'm growing, and not stagnant or shrinking."
– Jarod Kintz

"People live their lives bound by what they accept as correct and true. That's how they define Reality. But what does it mean to be "correct" or "true"? Merely vague concepts… Their Reality may all be a mirage. Can we consider them to simply be living in their own world, shaped by their beliefs?"
– Masashi Kishimoto

"I'd rather welcome change than cling to the past."
– Robert T. Kiyosaki

"You're only poor if you give up. The most important thing is that you did something. Most people only talk and dream of getting rich. You've done something."
– Robert T. Kiyosaki

"In school we learn that mistakes are bad, and we are punished for making them. Yet, if you look at the way humans are designed to learn, we learn by making mistakes. We learn to walk by falling down. If we never fell down, we would never walk."
– Robert T. Kiyosaki

"The human body has no more need for cows' milk than it does for dogs' milk, horses' milk, or giraffes' milk."
– Michael Klaper

"People who have attained things worth having in this world have worked while others have idled, have persevered while others gave up in despair, and have practiced early in life the valuable habits of self-denial, industry, and singleness of purpose. As a result, they

enjoy in later life the success often erroneously attributed to good luck."
– Grenville Kleiser

"I discovered I always have choices and sometimes it's only a choice of attitude."
– Judith M. Knowlton

"Great opportunities to help others seldom come, but small ones surround us every day."
– Sally Koch

"Courage is never to let your actions be influenced by your fears."
– Arthur Koestler

"Perhaps our greatest gift is helping people choose truly loving family, what we here in Hawaii call 'ohana — literally the circle of those who breathe together."
– Richard Koob

"She was fascinated with words. To her, words were things of beauty, each like a magical power or potion that could be combined with other words to create powerful spells."
– Dean Koontz

"One way to keep momentum going is to have constantly greater goals."
– Michael Korda

"You are here to live, not to sit on the couch."
– Jon Krakauer

"The devil is an optimist if he thinks he can make people meaner."
– Karl Kraus

"It is truth that liberates, not your effort to be free."
– Jiddu Krishnamurti

"We are raised on comparison; our education is based on it; so is our culture. So we struggle to be someone other than who we are."
– Jiddu Krishnamurti

"Meditation is not just the means to an end. It is both the means and the end."
– Jiddu Krishnamurti

"So when you are listening to somebody, completely, attentively, then you are listening not only to the words, but also to the feeling of what is being conveyed, to the whole of it, not part of it."
– Jiddu Krishnamurti

"Relationship is surely the mirror in which you discover yourself."
– Jiddu Krishnamurti

"Fear is what prevents the flowering of the mind."
– Jiddu Krishnamurti

"You can only be afraid of what you think you know."
– Jiddu Krishnamurti

"The moment you have in your heart this extraordinary thing called love and feel the depth, the delight, the ecstasy of it, you will discover that for you the world is transformed."
– Jiddu Krishnamurti

"The most beautiful people we have known are those who have known defeat, known suffering, known struggle, known loss, and have found their way out of the depths. These persons have an appreciation, a sensitivity, and an understanding of life that fills them with compassion, gentleness, and a deep loving concern. Beautiful people do not just happen."
– Elizabeth Kubler-Ross

"The opinion which other people have of you is their problem, not yours."
– Elisabeth Kubler-Ross

"Destiny is always a doorstep away, if we know to move in the right direction."
– Hari Kumar K

"When patterns are broken, new worlds emerge."
– Tuli Kupferberg

"When you are kind to others, it not only changes you, it changes the world."
– Harold Kushner

"You don't have to be religious to have a soul; everybody has one. You don't have to be religious to perfect your soul; I have found saintliness in avowed atheists."
– Harold Kushner

L

"A respectable appearance is sufficient to make people more interested in your soul."
– Karl Lagerfeld

"Don't look to the approval of others for your mental stability."
– Karl Lagerfeld

"The only way you get that fat off is to eat less and exercise more."
– Jack LaLanne

"To be kind, honest and have positive thoughts; to forgive those who harm us and treat everyone as a friend; to help those who are suffering and never to consider ourselves superior to anyone else: even if this advice seems rather simplistic, make the effort of seeing whether by following it you can find greater happiness."

– Dalai Lama (Tenzin Gyatso)

"In the past, oppressed peoples often resorted to violence in their struggle to be free. But visionaries such as Mahatma Gandi and the Reverend Martin Luther King, Jr. have shown us that successful changes can be brought about nonviolently. I believe that, at the basic human level, most of us wish to be peaceful. Deep down, we desire constructive, fruitful growth and dislike destruction.

Many people today agree that we need to reduce violence in our society. If we are truly serious about this, we must deal with the roots of violence, particularly those that exist within each of us. We need to embrace 'inner disarmament,' reducing our own emotions of suspicion, hatred, and hostility toward our brothers and sisters."

– Dalai Lama (Tenzin Gyatso)

"If you think that something small cannot make a difference, try going to sleep with a mosquito in the room."

– Dalai Lama (Tenzin Gyatso)

"Every day, think as you wake up, today I am fortunate to be alive, I have a precious human life, I am not going to waste it. I am going to use all my energies to develop myself, to expand my heart out to others; to achieve enlightenment for the benefit of all beings. I am going to have kind thoughts towards others, I am not going to get angry or think badly about others. I am going to benefit others as much as I can."

– Dalai Lama (Tenzin Gyatso)

"In the past, oppressed peoples often resorted to violence in their struggle to be free. But visionaries such as Mahatma Gandhi and the Rev. Martin Luther King Jr. have shown us that successful changes can be brought about nonviolently. I believe that, at the basic human level, most of us wish to be peaceful. Deep down, we desire constructive, fruitful growth and dislike destruction.

Many people today agree that we need to reduce violence in our society. If we are truly serious about this, we must deal with the roots of violence, particularly those that exist within each of us. We need to embrace 'inner disarmament,' reducing our own emotions of suspicion, hatred, and hostility toward our brothers and sisters."

– Dalai Lama (Tenzin Gyatso)

"As human beings we all want to be happy and free from misery. We have learned that the key to happiness is inner peace. The greatest obstacles to inner peace are disturbing emotions such as anger and attachment, fear and suspicion while love and compassion, a sense of universal responsibility are the sources of peace and happiness."

– Dalai Lama (Tenzin Gyatso)

"In the practice of tolerance, one's enemy is the best teacher."

– Dalai Lama (Tenzin Gyatso)

"If you want others to be happy, practice compassion. If you want to be happy, practice compassion."

– Dalai Lama (Tenzin Gyatso)

"Be kind whenever possible. It is always possible."
– Dalai Lama (Tenzin Gyatso)

"The key to happiness has nothing to do with belief in God, heaven, or spirituality. It has to be contentment and affection within oneself."
– Dalai Lama (Tenzin Gyatso)

"It is worth reminding ourselves that what brings us the greatest joy and satisfaction in life are those actions we undertake out of concern for others. Indeed we can go further. For whereas the fundamental questions of human existence, such as why we are here, where we are going, and whether the universe had a beginning, have each elicited different responses in different philosophical traditions, it is self-evident that a generous heart and wholesome actions lead to greater peace."
– Dalai Lama (Tenzin Gyatso)

"Religious people must do more than offer prayers if the world is to become a better place to live."
– Dalai Lama (Tenzin Gyatso)

"Forgiveness is letting go of all hope of a better past."
– Annie Lamont

"You have to make mistakes to find out who you aren't. You take the action, and the insight follows: You don't think your way into becoming yourself."
– Anne Lamott

"I would not sit waiting for some vague tomorrow, nor for something to happen. One could wait a lifetime, and find nothing at the end of the waiting. I would begin here, I would make something happen."
– Louis L'Amour

"Victory is won not in miles but in inches. Win a little now, hold your ground, and later win a little more."
– Louis L'Amour

"Start writing, no matter what. The water does not flow until the faucet is turned on."
– Louis L'Amour

"Somebody should tell us, right at the start of our lives, that we are dying. Then we might live life to the limit, every minute of every day."
– Michael Landon

"People who look ahead are very rare. Most people look to the past. We walk backwards, we back our way through life. We move forward but always while looking backwards. People who envision their future and more toward it, peering ahead are incredibly rare."
– Henri Langlois

"Respond intelligently even to unintelligent treatment."
– Laoze

"If the world seems cold to you, kindle fires to warm it."
– Lucy Larcom

"Believe in yourself and all that you are. Know that there is something inside you that is greater than any obstacle."
– Christian D. Larson

"Some of the world's greatest feats were accomplished by people not smart enough to know they were impossible."
– Doug Larson

"The world is full of people looking for spectacular happiness while they snub contentment."
– Doug Larson

"Life is ours to be spent, not to be saved."
– D. H. Lawrence

"The cosmos is a vast living body, of which we are still parts. The Sun is a great heart whose tremors run through our smallest veins. The moon is a great nerve-center from which we quiver forever. Who knows the power that Saturn has over us, or Venus? But it is a vital power, rippling exquisitely through us all the time."
– D. H. Lawrence

"All people dream; but not equally. Those who dream by night in the dusty recess of their minds wake in the day to find that it was vanity. But the dreamers of the day are the dangerous people, for they may act their dream with open eyes to make it possible."
– T.E. Lawrence

"There's a fine line between career criminals and career professionals because most of us fall somewhere in between."
– Samantha Leahy

"Any change, any loss, does not make us victims. Others can shake you, surprise you, disappoint you, but they can't prevent you from acting, from taking the situation you're presented with and moving on. No matter where you are in life, no matter what your

situation, you can always do something. You always have a choice and the choice can be power."
– Blaine Lee

"Adapt what is useful, reject what is useless, and add what is specifically your own."
– Bruce Lee

"The meaning of life is that it is to be lived, and it is not to be traded and conceptualized and squeezed into a patter of systems."
– Bruce Lee

"I cannot trust a man to control others who cannot control himself."
– Robert E. Lee

"Thoughts, like fleas, jump from man to man. But they don't bite everybody."
– Stanislaw Lec

"It is good to have an end to journey toward; but it is the journey that matters, in the end."
– Ursula K. Le Guin

"When nobody around you seems to measure up, it's time to check your yardstick."
– Bill Lemley

"We can't take any credit for our talents. It's how we use them that counts."
– Madeleine L'Engle

"You don't need anybody to tell you who you are or what you are. You are what you are!"
– John Lennon

"Reality leaves a lot to the imagination."
– John Lennon

"I've been fighting to be who I am all my life. What's the point of being who I am, if I can't have the person who was worth all the fighting for?"
– SD Lennox

"The greatest discovery of my generation is that we are unique. The greatest discovery of the next generation, I pray, is that we are one."
– Thomas Leonard

"One of the penalties of an ecological education is that one lives alone in a world of wounds."
– Aldo Leopold

"Only through our connectedness to others can we really know and enhance the self. And only through working on the self can we begin to enhance our connectedness to others."
– Harriet Goldhor Lerner

"The turning point in the process of growing up is when you discover the core strength within you that survives all hurt."
– Max Lerner

"The turning point in the process of growing up is when you discover the core strength within you that survives all hurt."
– Max Lerner

"What's terrible is to pretend that second-rate is first-rate. To pretend that you don't need love when you do; or you like your work when you know quite well you're capable of better."
– Doris Lessing

"We read to know we are not alone."
– C. S. Lewis

"Friendship is unnecessary, like philosophy, like art…. It has no survival value; rather it is one of those things which give value to survival."
– C.S. Lewis

"You are never too old to set another goal or to dream a new dream."
– C. S. Lewis

"Everybody is nine years old."
– Jerry Lewis

"Your opponent, in the end, is never really the player on the other side of the net, or the swimmer in the next lane, or the team on the other side of the field, or even the bar you must high-jump. Your opponent is yourself, your negative internal voices, your level of determination."
– Grace Lichtenstein

"The sinister, the terrible never deceive: the state in which they leave us is always one of enlightenment. And only this condition of vicious insight allows us a full grasp of the world, all things considered, just as a frigid melancholy grants us full possession of ourselves. We may hide from horror only in the heart of horror."
– Thomas Ligotti

"And in the end, it's not the years in your life that count. It's the life in your years."
– Abraham Lincoln

"Whatever you are, be a good one."
– Abraham Lincoln

"Love lasts when the relationship comes first."
– Abraham Lincoln

"Things may come to those who wait, but only the things left by those who hustle."
– Abraham Lincoln

"When I do good, I feel good; when I do bad, I feel bad, and that is my religion."
– Abraham Lincoln

"The most exhausting thing in life is being insecure."
– Anne Morrow Lindbergh

"As I have noticed on more than one occasion, life itself is unfair, and there is no complaint department, so we might as well accept things the way they happen, clean up the mess, and move on."
– Jeff Lindsay

"Things turn out best for the people who make the best of the way things turn out."
– Art Linkletter

"You cannot control the results, only your actions."
– Allan Lokos

"Once you learn to quit, it becomes a habit."
– Vince Lombardi

"The greatest accomplishment is not in never falling, but in rising again after you fall."
– Vince Lombardi

"I would rather be ashes than dust! I would rather that my spark should burn out in a brilliant blaze than it should be stifled by dry rot. I would rather be a superb meteor, every atom of me in magnificent glow, than a sleepy and permanent planet. The proper function of man is to live, not exist. I shall not waste my days in trying to prolong them, I shall use my time."
– Jack London

"We judge ourselves by what we feel capable of doing, while others judge us by what we have already done."
– Henry Wadsworth Longfellow

"Look not mournfully into the past, it comes not back again. Wisely improve the present, it is thine. Go forth to meet the shadowy future without fear and with a manly heart."
– Henry Wadsworth Longfellow

"The heights by great men reached and kept were not attained in sudden flight but, they while their companions slept, they were toiling upwards in the night."
– Henry Wadsworth Longfellow

"If you can't believe in miracles, then believe in yourself. When you want something bad enough, let that drive push you to make it happen. Sometimes you'll run into brick walls that are put there to test you. Find a way

around them and stay focused on your dream. Where there's a will, there's a way."
– Isabel Lopez

"No. Don't give up hope just yet. It's the last thing to go. When you have lost hope, you have lost everything. And when you think all is lost, when all is dire and bleak, there is always hope."
– Pittacus Lore

"When I dare to be powerful – to use my strength in the service of my vision – then it becomes less and less important whether or not I am afraid."
– Audre Lorde

"The only limits for tomorrow are the doubts we have today."
– Pittacus Lore

"When you are a mother, you are never really alone in your thoughts. A mother always has to think twice, once for herself and once for her child."
– Sophia Loren

"There is a fountain of youth: it is your mind, your talents, the creativity you bring to your life and the lives of people you love. When you learn to tap this source, you will truly have defeated age."
– Sophia Loren

"When I dare to be powerful – to use my strength in the service of my vision, then it becomes less and less important whether I am afraid."
– Audrey Lorde

"You've got to get up every morning with determination if you're going to go to bed with satisfaction."
– George Horace Lorimer

"Kind words are a creative force, a power that concurs in the building up of all that is good, and energy that showers blessings upon the world."
– Lawrence G. Lovasik

"Sometimes we understand grace only in retrospect. If someone were to ask me what grace is, I would probably respond, 'It's all grace.'"
– Bo Lozoff

"What we do see depends mainly on what we look for. In the same field the farmer will notice the crop, the geologists the fossils, botanists the flowers, artists the coloring, sportmen the cover for the game. Though we may all look at the same things, it does not all follow that we should see them."
– John Lubbock

"You change your life by changing your heart."
– Max Lucado

"Keep listening to music cause it gets you through everything, I promise."
– Mitch Lucker

"The kingdom of God is within you."
– Luke 17:21

"We won't always know whose lives we touched and made better for our having cared, because actions sometimes have unforeseen ramifications. What's important is that you do care and you act."
– Charlotte Lunsford

"For in the true nature of things, if we rightly consider, every green tree is far more glorious than if it were made of gold and silver."
– Martin Luther

"Knowledge is power only if man knows what facts not to bother with."
– Robert Staughton Lynd

"Most of us believe in trying to make other people happy only if they can be happy in ways which we approve."
– Robert Staughton Lynd

M

"There comes a time when humanity is called to shift to a new level of consciousness, to reach a higher moral ground. A time when we have to shed our fear and give hope to each other. That time is now."
– Wangari Maathai

"There is a life-affirming spark within you which constantly nudges you towards saying yes to life."
– Linda MacDonald

"Fear makes strangers of people who would be friends."
– Shirley MacLaine

"When we lose one we love, our bitterest tears are called forth by the memory of hours when we loved not enough."
– Maurice Maeterlinck

"I have never for one instant seen clearly within myself. How then would you have me judge the deeds of others?"
– Maurice Maeterlinck

"Being angry at the mistakes made by the heart will only leave you bitter."
– Jamie Magee

"It is true that we choose our life, but it's also true that we can choose at any moment to change our path."
– Jamie Magee

"Approval is overrated…Approval and disapproval alike satisfy those who deliver it more than those who receive it. I don't care for approval, and I don't mind doing without."
– Gregory Maguire

"Think clearly and deeply, go into the structure of your desires and their ramifications. They are a most important part of your mental and emotional make-up, and powerfully affect your actions."
– Nisargadatta Maharaj

"Remember, you cannot abandon what you do not know. To go beyond yourself, you must know yourself."
– Nisargadatta Maharaj

"The real does not die. The unreal never lived."
– Nisargadatta Maharaj

"It is always the false that makes you suffer, the false desires and fears, the false values and ideas, the false relationships between people. Abandon the false and you are free of pain; truth makes happy, truth liberates."
– Nisargadatta Maharaj

"Transforming yourself is a means of giving light to the whole world."
– Ramana Maharshi

"If you think you have it tough, read history books."
– Bill Maher

"Truth does not become more true by virtue of the fact that the entire world agrees with it, nor less so even if the whole world disagrees with it."
– Maimonides

"Without heroes, we are all plain people and don't know how far we can go."
– Bernard Malamud

"No matter how hard life is, don't lose hope."
– Zayn Malik

"An opinion should be the result of thought, not a substitute for it."
– Jef Mallett

"There is no greater weakness than stubbornness. If you cannot yield, if you cannot learn that there must be compromise in life – you lose."
– Maxwell Maltz

"People who say that life is not worthwhile are really saying that they themselves have no personal goals which are worthwhile. Get yourself a goal worth working for.

Better still, get yourself a project. Always have something ahead of you to look forward to, to work for and hope for."
– Maxwell Maltz

"Within you right now is the power to do things you never dreamed possible. This power becomes available to you just as you can change your beliefs."
– Maxwell Maltz

"The most delightful surprise in life is to suddenly recognize your own worth."
– Maxwell Maltz

"You must fight off a 'bad luck' way of thinking as if you were dealing with an invasion of hostile forces — for that is precisely what you are dealing with."
– Maxwell Maltz

"Sometimes it falls upon a generation to be great, you can be that generation"
– Nelson Mandela

"A winner is a dreamer who never gives up"
– Nelson Mandela

"As we are liberated from our own fear, our presence automatically liberates others."
– Nelson Mandela

"Remind thyself, in the darkest moments, that every failure is only a step toward success, every detection of what is false directs you toward what is true, every trial exhausts some tempting form of error, and every adversity will only hide, for a time, your path to peace and fulfillment. "
– Og Mandino

"I will waste not even a precious second today in anger or hate or jealousy or selfishness. I know that the seeds I sow I will harvest, because every action, good or bad, is always followed by an equal reaction. I will plant only good seeds this day."
– Og Mandino

"I seek constantly to improve my manners and graces, for they are the sugar to which all are attracted."
– Og Mandino

"I think you have to take charge of your own life and understand that you're either going to live somebody else's dream or live your own dream."
– Wilma Mankiller

"Doing nothing for others is the undoing of ourselves."
– Horace Mann

"Could we change our attitude, we should not only see life differently, but life itself would come to be different. Life would undergo a change of appearance because we ourselves had undergone a change of attitude."
– Katherine Mansfield

"Don't tell me about your god with your words. Show me about your god with your actions."
– Steve Maraboli

"If people refuse to look at you in a new light and they can only see you for what you were, only see you for the mistakes you've made, if they don't realize that you are not your mistakes, then they have to go."
– Steve Maraboli

"When in a relationship, a real man doesn't make his woman jealous of others, he makes others jealous of his woman."
— Steve Maraboli

"Life doesn't get easier or more forgiving, we get stronger and more resilient."
— Steve Maraboli

"Incredible change happens in your life when you decide to take control of what you do have power over instead of craving control over what you don't."
— Steve Maraboli

"Want to keep Christ in Christmas? Feed the hungry, clothe the naked, forgive the guilty, welcome the unwanted, care for the ill, love your enemies, and do unto others as you would have done unto you."
— Steve Maraboli

"Letting go means to come to the realization that some people are a part of your history, but not a part of your destiny."
— Steve Maraboli

"I want to be in a relationship where you telling me you love me is just a ceremonious validation of what you already show me."
— Steve Maraboli

"Everything changes when you start to emit your own frequency rather than absorbing the frequencies around you, when you start imprinting your intent on the universe rather than receiving an imprint from existence."
— Barbara Marciniak

"Deep within man dwell those slumbering powers; powers that would astonish him, that he never dreamed of possessing; forces that would revolutionize his life if aroused and put into action."
– Orison Swett Marden

"We lift ourselves by our thought. If you want to enlarge your life, you must first enlarge your thought of it and of yourself. Hold the ideal of yourself as you long to be, always everywhere."
– Orison Swett Marden

"Through fear of knowing who we really are we sidestep our own destiny, which leaves us hungry in a famine of our own making. We end up living numb, passionless lives, disconnected from our soul's true purpose. But when you have the courage to shape your life from the essence of who you are, you ignite, becoming truly alive."
– Dawna Markova

"Emancipate yourselves from mental slavery. None but ourselves can free our minds."
– Bob Marley

"Fortune sides with him who dares."
– Publius Vergillus "Virgil" Maro

"When a man tells you that he got rich through hard work, ask him: whose?"
– Don Marquis

"People trust their eyes above all else - but most people see what they wish to see, or what they believe they should see; not what is really there"
– Zoe Marriott

"Give to us clear vision that we may know where to stand and what to stand for — because unless we stand for something, we shall fall for anything."
– Peter Marshall

"Don't seek to merely get rid of the negative things in your life. Instead, transform their energy into something of real positive value."
– Ralph Marston

"A world of abundance surrounds you, if only you will step up and claim it. Make life happen through you rather than letting it happen to you. It will make all the difference in the world."
– Ralph Marston

"Let go of your attachment to being right, and suddenly your mind is more open. You're able to benefit from the unique viewpoints of others, without being crippled by your own judgment."
– Ralph Marston

"You must take life the way it comes at you and make the best of it."
– Yann Martel

"The young man and woman with sight sees things as they are. The young man and woman with insight, sees things as they could be."
– Joseph P. Martino

"A musician must make music, an artist must paint, a poet must write, if they are to be ultimately at peace with themselves. What a man can be, he must be."
– Abraham Maslow

"Is it easy? Usually not. But you don't forgive people for their benefit. You do it for your benefit."
– Andrew Matthews

"In this very breath that we take now lies the secret that all great teachers try to tell us."
– Peter Matthiessen

"To love someone is to see a miracle invisible to others."
– François Mauriac

"Often we allow ourselves to be upset by small things we should despise and forget. We lose many irreplaceable hours brooding over grievances that, in a year's time, will be forgotten by us and by everybody. Now, let us devote our life to worthwhile actions and feelings, to great thoughts, real affections, and enduring undertakings."
– Andre Maurois

"You don't have to be great to start – but you have to start to be great."
– John C. Maxwell

"If you do not express your own original ideas, if you do not listen to your own being, you will have betrayed yourself."
– Rollo May

"If you have a great ambition, take as big a step as possible in the direction of fulfilling it. The step may only be a tiny one, but trust that it may be the largest one possible for now."
– Mildred McAfee

"Every man needs love, guys like romance. I do anyway."
– Paul McCartney

"No other success can compensate for failure in the home."
– J.E. McCulloch

"We are the hurdles we leap to be ourselves."
– Michael McClure

"Pain and suffering are the soil of strength and courage."
– Lurlene McDaniel

"Do nothing, and nothing happens. Life is about decisions. You either make them or they're made for you, but you can't avoid them."
– Mhairi McFarlane

"A lot of what our brain does is synthesize a hallucination, a model of the world that we proceed to live in. This is a model reality, the real reality is completely unknowable."
– Dennis McKenna

"Suffering can be our greatest asset. If we have the capacity to learn from our suffering we have the capacity to improve our lives, improve our families, and improve our communities."
– Alexander McKinnon

"We have a calling. We are the people who know what we need. What we need surrounds us. What we need is each other. And when we act together, we will find our way."
– John McKnight

"We're constantly being told what other people think we are, and that's why it is so important to know yourself."
– Sarah McLachlan

"The poet, the artist, the sleuth - whoever sharpens our perception tends to be antisocial; rarely "well-adjusted", he cannot go along with currents and trends. A strange bond often exists between antisocial types in their power to see environments as they really are. This need to interface, to confront environments with a certain antisocial power is manifest in the famous story "The Emperor's New Clothes.""
– Marshall McLuhan

"The judgment of others does not change who I am. Quite the opposite is true. It reveals who they are. Those who deem me unworthy at a glance and pass me by, have my blessing to keep walking, for they have a long way to go. They have not reached the point where they are able to see and appreciate me for who I am."
– Terri McPherson

"The more severe the pain or illness, the more severe will be the necessary changes. These may involve breaking bad habits, or acquiring some new and better ones."
– Peter McWilliams

"We can not live only for ourselves. A thousand fibers connect us with our fellow men."
– Herman Melville

"A clergyman earns his living by assuring idiots that he can save them from an imaginary hell."
– Henry Louis Mencken

"The aim of public education is not to spread enlightenment at all: it is simply to reduce as many individuals as possible to the same safe level, to breed a standard citizenry, to put down dissent and originality."
– Henry Louis Mencken

"For every mess of asparagus that you eat, a human back somewhere must ache."
– Heny Louis Mencken

"Fears are educated into us, and can, if we wish, be educated out."
– Karl A. Menninger

"We stumble and fall constantly, even when we are most enlightened. But when we are in true spiritual darkness, we do not even know that we have fallen."
– Thomas Merton

"The whole idea of compassion is based on a keen awareness of the interdependence of all these living beings, which are all part of one another, and all involved in one another."
– Thomas Merton

"The beginning of love is to let those we love be perfectly themselves, and not to twist them to fit our own image. Otherwise we love only the reflection of ourselves we find in them."
– Thomas Merton

"One mistake does not have to rule a person's entire life."
– Joyce Meyer

"Productivity is never an accident. It is always the result of a commitment to excellence, intelligent planning, and focused effort."
– Paul J. Meyer

"It's not the face, but the expressions on it. It's not the voice, but what you say. It's not how you look in that body, but the thing you do with it. You are beautiful."
– Stephenie Meyer

"I saw the angel in the marble and carved until I set him free."
– Michelangelo

"Each one of us can make a difference. Together we make change."
– Barbara Mikulski

"I never suspected that I would have to learn how to live — that there were specific disciplines and ways of seeing the world I had to master before I could awaken to a simple, happy, uncomplicated life."
– Dan Millman

"All young people, regardless of sexual orientation or identity, deserve a safe and supportive environment in which to achieve their full potential."
– Harvey Milk

"One person with a belief is equal to a force of 99 who have only interests."
– John Stuart Mill

"One's destination is never a place, but a new way of seeing things."
– Henry Miller

"The world is not to be put in order; the world is order incarnate. It is for us to harmonize with this order."
– Henry Miller

"The moment one gives close attention to anything, even a blade of grass, it becomes a mysterious, awesome, indescribably magnificent world in itself."
– Henry Miller

"The aim of life is to live, and to live means to be aware, joyously, drunkenly, serenely, divinely aware."
– Henry Miller

"Life moves on, whether we act as cowards or heroes. Life has no other discipline to impose, if we would but realize it, than to accept life unquestioningly. Everything we shut our eyes to, everything we run away from, everything we deny, denigrate or despise, serves to defeat us in the end. What seems nasty, painful, evil, can become a source of beauty, joy, and strength, if faced with an open mind. Every moment is a golden one for him who has the vision to recognize it as such"
– Henry Miller

"Everyone has his own reality in which, if one is not too cautious, timid or frightened, one swims. This is the only reality there is."
– Henry Miller

"You probably wouldn't worry about what people think of you if you could know how seldom they do."
– Olin Miller

"The mind is its own place, and in itself, can make a heaven of hell, a hell of heaven."
– John Milton

"Many of us are slaves to our minds. Our own mind is our worst enemy. We try to focus, and our mind wanders off. We try to keep stress at bay, but anxiety keeps us awake at night. We try to be good to the people we love, but then we forget them and put ourselves first. And when we want to change our life, we dive into spiritual practice and expect quick results, only to lose focus after the honeymoon has worn off. We return to our state of bewilderment. We're left feeling helpless and discouraged. It seems we all agree that training the body through exercise, diet, and relaxation is a good idea, but why don't we think about training our minds?"
– Sakyong Mipham

"I see music as fluid architecture."
– Joni Mitchell

"Maybe love is like luck. You have to go all the way to find it."
– Robert Mitchum

"A lie has speed, but truth has endurance."
– Edgar J. Mohn

"'What are you?' someone asks. 'I am the story of myself,' comes the answer."
– M. Scott Momady

"When something hard comes along. A man steps up. He doesn't dodge it or run away from it or try to push it onto someone else. He steps up. Even if it isn't his responsibility. And that's why there are so many guys and so few men. Because stepping up is hard."
– Ben Monopoli

"It's all make believe, isn't it?"
– Marilyn Monroe

"Success makes so many people hate you. I wish it wasn't hat way. It would be wonderful to enjoy success without seeing envy in the eyes of those around you."
– Marilyn Monroe

"Every human being is a problem in search of a solution."
– Ashley Montagu

"I am afraid that our eyes are bigger than our stomachs, and that we have more curiosity than understanding. We grasp at everything, but catch nothing except wind."
– Michel de Montaigne

"The greatest thing in the world is to know how to belong to oneself."
– Michel de Montaigne

"I do not care so much what I am to others as I care what I am to myself."
– Michel de Montaigne

"Well, we all make mistakes, dear, so just put it behind you. We should regret our mistakes and learn from them, but never carry them forward into the future with us."
– L.M. Montgomery

"Everybody is special. Everybody. Everybody is a hero, a lover, a fool, a villain. Everybody. Everybody has their story to tell."
– Alan Moore

"Education is not the piling on of learning, information, data, facts, skills, or abilities – that's training or instruction – but is rather making visible what is hidden as a seed."
– Thomas More

"For if you suffer your people to be ill-educated, and their manners to be corrupted from their infancy, and then punish them for those crimes to which their first education disposed them, what else is to be concluded from this, but that you first make thieves and then punish them."
– Thomas More

"As knowledge increases, wonder deepens."
– Charles Morgan

"The first step towards getting somewhere is to decide that you are not going to stay where you are."
– John Pierpont Morgan

"You may tell a tale that takes up residence in someone's soul, becomes their blood and self and purpose. That tale will move them and drive them and who knows that they might do because of it, because of your words. That is your role, your gift."
– Erin Morgenstern

"The most important kind of freedom is to be what you really are. You trade in your reality for a role. You trade in your sense for an act. You give up your ability to feel, and in exchange, put on a mask. There can't be any large-scale revolution until there's a personal revolution, on an individual level. It's got to happen inside first."
– Jim Morrison

"Start living now. Stop saving the good china for that special occasion. Stop withholding your love until that special person materializes. Every day you are alive is a special occasion. Every minute, every breath, is a gift from God."
– Mary Manin Morrisse

"You don't have to make something that people call art. Living is an artistic activity, there is an art to getting through the day."
– Viggo Mortensen

"Life is what we make of it, always has been, always will be."
– Anna Mary Robertson "Grandma" Moses

"Neither a lofty degree of intelligence nor imagination nor both together go to the making of genius. Love, love, love, that is the soul of genius."
– Wolfgang Amadeus Mozart

"You're not obligated to win. You're obligated to keep trying. To the best you can do everyday."
– Jason Mraz

"It's strange how dreams get under your skin and give your heart a test for what's real and what's imaginary."
– Jason Mraz

"Frustration and Love can't exist in the same place at the same time, so get real and start doing what you would rather be doing in life. Love your life. All of it. Even the heavy shit that happened to you when you were 8. All of it was and IS perfect."
– Jason Mraz

"Thousands of tired, nerve-shaken, over-civilized people are beginning to find out going to the mountains is going home; that wilderness is a necessity."
– John Muir

"Everybody needs beauty as well as bread, places to play in and pray in, where nature may heal and give strength to body and soul."
– John Muir

"Can you see the power emotion has to distort our outlook? Makes you wonder, did you have a bad day, or did you make it a bad day?"
– Brandon Mull

"Life is divine, life is an extraordinary, incredible, miraculous phenomenon, our most precious gift. We must grow a global brain, a global heart, and global soul. That is our most pressing current evolutionary task."
– Robert Muller

"Use every letter you write, every conversation you have, every meeting you attend, to express your fundamental beliefs and dreams. Affirm to others the vision of the world you want. You are a free, immensely powerful source of life and goodness. Affirm it. Spread it. Radiate it. Think day and night about it and you will see a miracle happen: the greatness of our own life."
– Robert Muller

"What I do today is important because I am exchanging a day of my life for it."
– Hugh Mulligan

"If you're not happy in life then you need to change, calibrate, readjust...flush your negative energy and fill it with positive energy; How do we do that you might ask?

Well I would start by making others happy, diseases are not the only thing that spreads easy. We are all connected in some form of unseen energy... think how those around you will impact you and make you feel if they were happy?"
– Al Munoz

"The secret of your future is hidden in your daily routine."
– Mike Murdock

"We sometimes have a flash of understanding that amounts to the insight of genius, and yet it slowly withers, even in our hands - like a flower. The form remains, but the colours and the fragrance are gone."
– Robert Musil

"My theory is that all of Scottish cuisine is based on a dare."
– Mike Myers

N

"You don't read Gatsby, I said, to learn whether adultery is good or bad but to learn about how complicated issues such as adultery and fidelity and marriage are. A great novel heightens your senses and sensitivity to the complexities of life and of individuals, and prevents you from the self-righteousness that sees morality in fixed formulas about good and evil."
– Azar Nafisi

"Things derive their being and nature by mutual dependence and are nothing in themselves."
– Natgarjuna

"A tornado of thought is unleashed after each new insight. This in turn results in an earthquake of assumptions. These are natural disasters that re-shape the spirit."
– Vera Nazarian

"Love, far from being blind, is the very emotion that allows us to see."
– Cristina Nehring

"We live in a wonderful world that is full of beauty, charm and adventure. There is no end to the adventures that we can have if only we seek them with our eyes open."
– Jawaharlal Nehru

"Sexuality expresses God's intention that people find authentic humanness not in isolation but in relationship."
– James B. Nelson

"Look within. The secret is inside you."
– Hui Neng

"What others are doing or accomplishing is irrelevant to your growth."
– Janet Gallagher Nestor

"Nothing would be done at all if a man waited until he could do it so well that no one could find fault with it."
– John Henry Newman

"Even if it's absurd to think you can change things, it's even more absurd to believe that it is foolish and unimportant to try."
– Peter C. Newman

"Much of the conflict of our lives can be explained by one simple but unhappy fact: We don't really listen to each other."
– Michael P. Nichols

"Remain true to the earth, my brethren, with the power of your virtue! Let your bestowing love and your knowledge be devoted to be the meaning of the earth! Thus do I pray and conjure you."
– Friedrich Nietzsche

"It is not a lack of love, but a lack of friendship that makes unhappy marriages."
– Friedrich Wilhelm Nietzsche

"Dancing in all its forms cannot be excluded from the curriculum of all noble education; dancing with the feet, with ideas, with words, and, need I add that one must also be able to dance with the pen?"
– Friedrich Nietzsche

"Gracefulness belongeth to the munificence of the magnanimous – but precisely to the hero is beauty the hardest thing of all. Unattainable is beauty by all ardent wills. A little more, a little less: precisely this is much here, it is the most here. To stand with relaxed muscles and with unharnessed will: that is the hardest for all of you, ye sublime ones! When power becometh gracious and descendeth into the visible – I call such condescension, beauty."
– Friedrich Nietzsche

"Success is the progressive realization of a worthy ideal."
– Earl Nightengale

"Your world is a living expression of how you are using and have used your mind."
– Earl Nightingale

"Throughout all history, the great wise men and teachers, philosophers, and prophets have disagreed with one another on many different things. It is only on this one point that they are in complete and unanimous agreement. We become what we think about."
– Earl Nightingale

"I think one's feelings waste themselves in words; they ought all to be distilled into actions which bring results."
– Florence Nightingale

"Dreams pass into the reality of action. From the actions stems the dream again; and this interdependence produces the highest form of living."
– Anais Nin

"The personal life deeply lived always expands into truths beyond itself."
– Anais Nin

"When we blindly adopt a religion, a political system, a literary dogma, we become automatons."
– Anais Nin

"If I have been of service, if I have glimpsed more of the nature and essence of ultimate good, if I am inspired to reach wider horizons of thought and action, if I am at peace with myself, it has been a successful day."
– Alex Nobel

"There are many things in life that will catch your eye, but only a few will catch your heart. Pursue those."
– Michael Nolan

"A lot of what passes for depression these days is nothing more than a body saying that it needs work."
– Geoffrey Norman

"Dreams are illustrations from the book your soul is writing about you."
– Marsha Norman

"This is the way of peace: Overcome evil with good, falsehood with truth, and hatred with love."
– Mildred "Peace Pilgrim" Norman

"There is a spark of good in everybody, no matter how deeply it may be buried, it is there. It's waiting to govern your life gloriously."
– Mildred "Peace Pilgrim" Norman

"One little person, giving all of her time to peace, makes news. Many people, giving some of their time, can make history."
– Mildred "Peace Pilgrim" Norman

"It's no coincidence that four of the six letters in health are 'heal.'"
– Ed Northstrum

"In my friend, I find a second self."
– Isabel Norton

"To live a spiritual life we must first find the courage to enter into the desert of loneliness and to change it by gentle and persistent efforts into a garden of solitude."
– Henri J. M. Nouwen

"Granted that I must die, how shall I live?"
– Michael Novak

"Reading is the sole means by which we slip, involuntarily, often helplessly, into another's skin, another's voice, another's soul."
– Joyce Carol Oates

"All I ask is one thing, and I'm asking this particularly of young people: please don't be cynical. I hate cynicism, for the record, it's my least favorite quality and it doesn't lead anywhere. Nobody in life gets exactly what they thought they were going to get. But if you work really hard and you're kind, amazing things will happen."
– Conan O'Brien

"We don't accomplish anything in this world alone. And whatever happens is the result of the whole tapestry of one's life and all the weavings of individual threads from one to another that creates something."
– Sandra Day O'Connor

"May you experience each day as a sacred gift woven around the heart of wonder."
– John O'Donohue

"Your identity is not equivalent to your biography. There is a place in you where you have never been wounded, where there's a seamlessness in you, and where there is a confidence and tranquility."
– John O'Donohue -

"I have already settled it for myself so flattery and criticism go down the same drain and I am quite free."
– Georgia O'Keeffe

"The most authentic thing about us is our capacity to create, to overcome, to endure, to transform, to love, and to be greater than our suffering."
– Ben Okri

"The whole idea is to earn the flavor. No one gives it to you."
– Jamie Oliver

"Find the things that matter, and hold on to them, and fight for them, and refuse to let them go."
– Lauren Oliver

"One day you finally knew what you had to do, and began, though the voices around you kept shouting their bad advice."
– Mary Oliver

"Your time is way too valuable to be wasting on people that can't accept who you are."
– Turcois Ominek

"The invitation is about participation, not mere observation. We are not journeying in the universe but with the universe. We are not concerned about living in an evolving world but co-evolving with our world. We are parts of a whole, much greater than the sum of its parts, and yet within each part we are interconnected with the whole."
– Diarmuid O'Murchu

"Healing yourself is connected with healing others."
– Yoko Ono

"You can't be conferred with a glory you never configured your mind to come to."
– Ifeanyi Enoch Onuoha

"A compliment is verbal sunshine."
– Robert Orben

"I may be a living legend, but that sure don't help when I've got to change a flat tire."
– Roy Orbison

"Always read something that will make you look good if you die in the middle of it."
– P. J. O'Rourke

"The planet does not need more 'successful' people. But it does desperately need more peacemakers, healers, restorers, storytellers, and lovers of every shape and form. It needs people who live well in their places. It needs people of moral courage willing to join the fight to

make the world habitable and humane. And these needs have little to do with success as our culture has defined it."
– David Orr

"Creativity is a flower that praise brings to bloom, but discouragement often nips in the bud."
– Alex F. Osborn

"When plans are laid in advance, it is surprising how often the circumstances fit in with them."
– William Osler

"You are stronger than you know."
– Lori Osterman

"In science the credit goes to the man who convinces the world, not to the man to whom the idea first occurs."
– William Osler

"Change and growth take place when a person has risked himself and dares to become involved with experimenting with his own life."
– Herbert Otto

"When one realizes one is asleep, at that moment one is already half-awake."
– P. D. Ouspensky

"Everything can change in a heartbeat; it can slip away in an instant. Everything you trust, and treasure, whatever brings you comfort, comes at a terrible cost. Health is temporary; money disappears. Safety is nothing big an illusion.
So when the moment comes, and everything you depend upon changes, or perhaps someone you love

disappears, or no longer loves you, must disaster follow? Or will you-somehow-adapt?"
– Margaret Overton

"Dripping water hollows out stone, not through force but through persistence."
– Ovid

"Great talents, by the rust of disuse grow lethargic and shrink from what they were."
– Ovid

P

"No matter how many people believe or don't believe in you, you must be the ultimate believer in yourself!"
– Pablo

"Don't look back. Something may be gaining on you."
– Satchel Paige

"Such is the irresistible nature of truth, that all it asks, and all it wants, is the liberty of appearing."
– Thomas Paine

"Yes, terrible things happen, but sometimes those terrible things- they save you."
– Chuck Palahniuk

"You buy furniture. You tell yourself, this is the last sofa I will ever need in my life. Buy the sofa, then for a couple years you're satisfied that no matter what goes wrong, at least you've got your sofa issue handled. Then the right set of dishes. Then the perfect bed. The drapes. The rug. Then you're trapped in your lovely nest, and the things you used to own, now they own you."
– Chuck Palahniuk

"The voice says, maybe you don't go to hell for the things you do. Maybe you go to hell for the things you don't do. The things you don't finish."
– Chuck Palahniuk

"If you repeatedly go out there, and you are the change that you want to see, then that's what you are."
– Keke Palmer

"We are participants in a vast communion of being, and if we open ourselves to its guidance, we can learn anew how to live in this great and gracious community of truth."
– Parker Palmer

"Books, which we mistake for consolation, only add depth to our sorrow."
– Orhan Pamuk

"Live in the present, remember the past, and fear not the future, for it doesn't exist and never shall. There is only now."
– Christopher Paolini

"Limitations live only in our minds. But if we use our imaginations, our possibilities become limitless."
– Jamie Paolinetti

"If you don't live it, it won't come out of your horn."
– Charlie Parker

"Memories of our lives, of our works, and our deeds will continue in others."
– Rosa Parks

"A good coach will make his players see what they can be rather than what they are."
– Ara Parsegian

"If you don't like the road you're walking, start paving another one."
– Dolly Parton

"Kind words do not cost much. They never blister the tongue or lips. They make other people good-natured. They also produce their own image on men's souls, and a beautiful image it is."
– Blaise Pascal

"Let me tell you the secret that has led me to my goal: my strength lies solely in my tenacity."
– Louis Pasteur

"When you are inspired by some great purpose, some extraordinary project, all your thoughts break their bonds; your mind transcends limitations, your consciousness expands in every direction, and you find yourself in a new, great and wonderful world. Dormant forces, faculties and talents become alive, and you

discover yourself to be a greater person by far than you ever dreamed yourself to be."
— Patanjali

"Be a ladder, not a leader."
— Jayesh Patel

"The secret of discipline is motivation. When a man is sufficiently motivated, discipline will take care of itself."
— Alexander Paterson

"Be not forgetful to entertain strangers for thereby some have entertained angels unawares."
— Paul of Tarsus

"When you're screwing up and nobody says anything to you anymore, that means they've given up on you."
— Randy Pausch

"People think I'm disciplined. It is not discipline. It is devotion. There is a great difference."
— Luciano Pavarotti

"Life is pain and the enjoyment of love is an anesthetic."
— Cesare Pavese

"It was impossible to understand how brief it is. It seemed like youth would last so long; it would last forever. But it's just a blink."
— Chris Pavone

"When you're good at something, you'll tell everyone. When you're great at something, they'll tell you."
— Walter Payton

"Paint the walls of your mind with many beautiful pictures."
– William Lyons Phelps

"Finally, brethren, whatever is true, whatever is honorable, whatever is right, whatever is pure, whatever is lovely, whatever is of good repute, if there is any excellence and if anything is worthy of praise, let your mind dwell on these things."
– Phillipians 4:8

"Do not speak your happiness to one less fortunate than yourself."
– Plutarch

"For as he thinketh in his heart, so is he."
– Psalms 23:7

"There is a basic law that like attracts like. Negative-thinking definitely attracts negative results. Conversely, if a person habitually thinks optimistically and hopefully his positive-thinking sets in motion creative forces – and success instead of eluding him flows toward him."
– Norman Vincent Peale

"When you get up in the morning, you have two choices – either to be happy or to be unhappy. Just choose to be happy"
– Norman Vincent Peale

"Live your life and forget your age."
– Norman Vincent Peale

"Be so strong that nothing can disturb your peace of mind. Talk health, happiness, and prosperity to every person you meet. Make all your friends feel there is something special in them. Look at the sunny side of

everything. Think only the best, be as enthusiastic about the success of others as you are about your own. Forget the mistakes of the past and press on to the greater achievements of the future. Give everyone a smile. Spend so much time improving yourself that you have no time left to criticize others. Be too big for worry and too noble for anger."
– Norman Vincent Peale

"Change your thoughts, and you change your world."
– Norman Vincent Peale

"Do you know what a big shot is? A little shot who keeps shooting."
– Norman Vincent Peale

"The objectives of two lovers is almost always the same: to find meaning in their individual lives and in their life together."
– Paul Pearsall

"Heroes take journeys, confront dragons, and discover the treasure of their true selves."
– Carol Pearson

"Ultimately, we are all products of the experiences we have and the decisions we make as children, and it remains a peculiar detail of the human condition that something as precious as a future is entrusted to us when we possess so little foresight. Perhaps that's what makes hindsight so intriguing. When you're young the future is a blank canvas, but looking back you are always able to see the big picture."
– Simon Pegg

"What disappoints me the most is somebody who can do something well and does not do it."
– Sean Penn

"Turning one's back on stardom might be the highest form of common sense. One that I would aspire to be more complete with."
– Sean Penn

"In all debates, let truth be thy aim, not victory, or an unjust interest."
– William Penn

"I'll take character over reputation. Your character is what you really are, while your reputation is merely what others think you are."
– AJ Perez

"What you leave behind is not what is engraved in stone monuments, but what is woven into the lives of others."
– Pericles

"When we give our energy to a different dream, the world is transformed. To create a new world, we must first create a new dream."
– John Perkins

"It doesn't matter if a million people tell you what you can't do, or if ten million tell you no. If you get one yes from God that's all you need."
– Tyler Perry

"What you leave behind is not what is engraved in stone monuments, but what is woven into the lives of others."
– Pericles

"We consume our tomorrows fretting about our yesterdays."
– Persius

"Biochemicals are the physiological substrates of emotion, the molecular underpinnings of what we experience as feelings, sensations, thoughts, drives, perhaps even spirit or soul."
– Candace B. Pert

"Speak when you are angry, and you'll make the best speech you'll ever regret."
– Laurence J. Peter

"The art of awareness is the art of learning how to wake up to the eternal miracle of life with its limitless possibilities."
– Wilfred Peterson

"Jealousy is the lock that closes your heart, understanding is the key that opens it."
– Ken Petti

"Time is a companion that goes with us on a journey. It reminds us to cherish each moment, because it will never come again. What we leave behind is not as important as how we have lived."
– Jean Luc Picard

"I am always doing that which I cannot do in order that I may learn how to do it."
– Pablo Picasso

"Love is the greatest refreshment in life."
– Pablo Picasso

"Art washes away from the soul the dust of everyday life."
– Pablo Picasso

"Art is a lie that makes us realize truth."
– Pablo Picasso

"If you have made mistakes, even serious ones, there is always another chance for you. What we call failure is not the falling down, but the staying down."
– Mary Pickford

"If you realized how powerful your thoughts are, you would never think a negative thought."
– Peace Pilgrim

"The place to improve the world is first in one's own heart and head and hands, and then work outward from there."
– Robert M. Pirsig

"The truth knocks on the door and you say, 'Go away, I'm looking for the truth,' and so it goes away. Puzzling."
– Robert M. Pirsig

"You start getting into trouble in life when you start comparing and contrasting your life to anyone else's. You don't win when you do that."
– Jeremy Pivin

"All matter originates and exists only by virtue of a force which brings the particle of an atom to vibration."
– Max Planck

"Hurl yourself at goals above your head and bear the lacerations that come when you slip and make a fool of yourself. Try always, as long as you have breath in your body, to take the hard way – and work, work, work to build yourself into a rich, continually evolving entity."
– Sylvia Plath

"As youth fades and time brings changes, we may change many of our present opinions. O let us refrain from setting ourselves up as judge of the highest matters."
– Plato

"Life must be lived as play."
– Plato

"Wise men speak because they have something to say; fools, because they have to say something."
– Plato

"The man who makes everything that leads to happiness depend upon himself, and not upon other men, has adopted the very best plan for living happily."
– Plato

"We can easily forgive a child who is afraid of the dark. The real tragedy of life is when men are afraid of the light."
– Plato

"Lack of activity destroys the good condition of every human being, while movement and methodical physical exercise save it and preserve it."
– Plato

"We neglect those things which are under our very eyes, and heedless of things within our grasp, pursue those which are afar off."
– Pliny the Elder

"What we achieve inwardly will change outer reality."
– Plutarch

"The best things in life make you sweaty."
– Edgar Allan Poe

"It is by no means an irrational fancy that, in a future existence, we shall look upon what we think our present existence as a dream."
– Edgar Allen Poe

"The best relationships in our lives are the best not because they have been the happiest ones, they are that way because they have stayed strong through the most tormentful of storms."
– Pandora Poikilos

"No matter how small and unimportant what we are doing may seem, if we do it well, it may soon become the step that will lead us to better things."
– Channing Pollock

"They dream in courtship, but in wedlock wake."
– Alexander Pope

"Anyone who is steady in his determination for the advanced stage of spiritual realization and can equally tolerate the onslaughts of distress and happiness is certainly a person eligible for liberation."
– A.C. Bhaktivedanta Swami Prabhupada

"Truth is like the sun. You can shut it out for a time, but it ain't goin' away."
– Elvis Presley

"The world is round and the place which may seem like the end may also be the beginning."
– Ivy Baker Priest

"Flowers will lean around walls to reach the sunlight."
– Jeff Primack

"Let us be grateful for people who make us happy. They are the charming gardeners who make your souls blossom."
– Marcel Proust

"There is no man, however wise, who has not at some period of his youth said things, or lived in a way the consciousness of which is so unpleasant to him in later life that he would gladly, if he could, expunge it from his memory."
– Marcel Proust

"Every reader finds himself. The writer's work is merely a kind of optical instrument that makes it possible for the reader to discern what, without this book, he would perhaps never have seen in himself."
– Marcel Proust

"Let us be grateful to people who make us happy; they are the charming gardeners who make our souls blossom."
– Marcel Proust

"You can't turn back the clock. But you can wind it up again."
– Bonnie Prudden

"If you want something you can have it, but only if you want everything that goes with it, including all the hard work and the despair, and only if you're willing to risk failure. "
– Philip Pullman

"We don't need a list of rights and wrongs, tables of dos and don'ts: we need books, time, and silence. *Thou shalt not* is soon forgotten, but *Once upon a time* lasts forever."
– Phillip Pullman

"The differences between optimists and extreme optimists are remarkable, and suggest that over-optimism, like overconfidence, may in fact lead to behaviors that are unwise."
– Manju Puri

"You've gotta dance like there's nobody watching. Love like you'll never be hurt. Sing like there's nobody listening. And live like it's heaven on earth."
– William W. Purkey

"A lawyer with a briefcase can steal more than a hundred men with guns."
– Mario Puzo

"Your present circumstances don't determine where you can go; they merely determine where you start."
– Nido Qubein

R

"A man's dreams are an index to his greatness."
– Zadok Rabinowitz

"Live with intention. Walk to the edge. Listen hard. Practice wellness. Play with abandon. Laugh. Choose with no regret. Appreciate your friends. Continue to learn. Do what you love. Live as if this is all there is."
– Mary Ann Radmacher

"I think dogs are the most amazing creatures; they give unconditional love. For me, they are the role model for being alive."
– Gilda Radner

"Show by your lives that religion does not mean words, or names, or sects, but that it means spiritual realization."
– Sri Ramakrishna

"What we achieve inwardly will change outer reality."
– Otto Rank

"The insights we receive when going silent, it's our gift to ourselves. Returning and living them, sharing them, that is our gift to the world."
– Kamal Ravikant

"Your past is not who you are, it's who you were."
– James Ray

"Begin doing what you want to do now. We have only this moment, sparkling like a star in our hand, and melting like a snowflake."
– Marie Ray

"Courage is not the absence of fear, but rather the judgment that something else is more important than fear."
– Ambrose Redmoon

"There is, within each of us, a heart that is much larger than ordinary human affairs would normally reveal, a heart that can embrace the world because it overflows with love."
– Julie Redstone

"There are patterns in everything, in the whole of Nature, from the way the stars turn in the heavens to the whorl of a shell or the petals of a flower and the way leaves arrange themselves about a twig. There are forces, hidden forces. If I can discover what they are, how they

operate, I will have my hands upon the levers of creation and can work them myself."
– Celia Rees

"Healing is not a matter of technique or mechanism; it is a work of spirit."
– Rachel Naomi Remen

"Healing may not be so much about getting better, as about letting go of everything that isn't you – all of the expectations, all of the beliefs – and becoming who you are."
– Rachel Naomi Remen

"It's not how old you are, it's how you are old."
– Jules Renard

"I would much rather have regrets about not doing what people said, than regretting not doing what my heart led me to and wondering what life had been like if I'd just been myself."
– Brittany Renée

"I experience a period of frightening clarity in those moments when nature is so beautiful. I am no longer sure of myself, and the paintings appear as in a dream. An artist, under pain of oblivion, must have confidence in himself, and listen only to his real master: Nature."
– Auguste Renoir

"Dare to reach out your hand into the darkness, to pull another hand into the light."
– Norman B. Rice

"There must be those among whom we can sit down and weep and still be counted as warriors."
– Adrienne Rich

"One of the great lessons I've learned in athletics is that you've got to discipline your life. No matter how good you may be, you've got to be willing to cut out of your life those things that keep you from going to the top."
– Bob Richards

"Don't be fooled by the calendar. There are only as many days in the year as you make use of. One man gets only a week's value out of a year while another man gets a full year's value out of a week.
– Charles Richards

"Let no one be deluded that a knowledge of the path can substitute for putting one foot in front of the other."
– Mary Caroline Richards

"Do not wait for extraordinary circumstances to do good action; try to use ordinary situations."
– Jean Paul Richter

"I live my life in widening circles that reach out across the world."
– Rainer Maria Rilke

"I hold this to be the highest task for a bond between two people: that each protect the solitude of the other."
– Rainer Maria Rilke

"You live in illusion and the appearance of things. There is a reality, but you don't know this. When you understand this you will see that you are nothing. And being nothing, you are everything. That is all."
– Kalu Rinpoche

"Whenever catching sight of others, look on them with an open, loving heart."
– Patrul Rinpoche

"But remember, boy, that a kind act can sometimes be as powerful as a sword."
– Rick Riordan

"Like the in breath and the out breath. You gather the light and then you give it out. That's just the way it works."
– Nancy Rivard

"If you don't set a baseline standard for what you'll accept in life, you'll find it's easy to slip into behaviors and attitudes or a quality of life that's far below what you deserve."
– Anthony Robbins

"With our minds we can make anything happen. I believe in immersion – it's one thing to know the principals and it's another thing to live it day to day so it becomes a pattern"
– Anthony Robbins

"I saw a study that the more television people watched, the more afraid of their neighbors they became. The researchers called it 'the dangerous world syndrome.' The mathematical correspondence was compelling. The more television people watched, the more crime they thought there was in their neighborhood, and the more exaggerated their belief about how many murders and burglaries were taking place."
– John Robbins

"If we encourage and uphold our essential goodness and capacity for loving connection, we can nurture a society of people who are healthy and whole and whose lives will bring healing, peace, and joy to those they touch."
– John Robbins

"Sounds travel through space long after their wave patterns have ceased to be detectable by the human ear: some cut right through the ionosphere and barrel on out into the cosmic heartland, while others bounce around, eventually being absorbed into the vibratory fields of earthly barriers, but in neither case does the energy succumb; it goes on forever - which is why we, each of us, should take pains to make sweet notes."
– Tom Robbins

"I don't believe that the solutions in society will come from the left or the right or the north or the south. They will come from islands within those organizations, islands of people with integrity who want to do something."
– Karl-Henrik Robert

"If you don't go after what you want, you'll never have it. If you don't ask, the answer is always no. If you don't step forward, you're always in the same place."
– Nora Roberts

"We win by tenderness. We conquer by forgiveness."
– Frederick William Robertson

"Our ability to look back on the past, our need or desire to make sense of it, is both a blessing and a curse; and our inability to see into the future with any degree of

accuracy is, simultaneously, the thing that saves us and the thing that condemns us."
– James Robertson

"Nobody can go back and start a new beginning, but anyone can start today and make a new ending."
– Maria Robinson

"Cynicism is what passes for insight when courage is lacking."
– Anita Roddick

"The good life is a process, not a state of being. It is a direction, not a destination."
– Carl Rogers

"Mutual caring relationships require kindness and patience, tolerance, optimism, joy in the other's achievements, confidence in oneself, and the ability to give without undue thought of gain."
– Fred Rogers

"Anything that's human is mentionable, and anything that is mentionable can be more manageable. When we can talk about our feelings, they become less overwhelming, less upsetting, and less scary. The people we trust with that important talk can help us know that we are not alone."
– Fred Rogers

"We need to help people to discover the true meaning of love. Love is generally confused with dependence. Those of us who have grown in true love know that we can love only in proportion to our capacity for independence."
– Fred Rogers

"Everyone longs to be loved. And the greatest thing we can do is to let people know that they are loved and capable of loving."
– Fred Rogers

"The best way out of a difficulty is through it."
– Will Rogers

"You must constantly ask yourself these questions: Who am I around? What are they doing to me? What have they got me reading? What have they got me saying? Where do they have me going? What do they have me thinking? And most important, what do they have me becoming? Then ask yourself the big question: Is that okay?"
– E. James Rohn

"We must all suffer one of two things: the pain of discipline or the pain of regret or disappointment."
– E. James Rohn

"Scar tissue is stronger than regular tissue. Realize the strength, move on."
– Henry Rollins

"Sometimes the truth hurts, and sometimes it feels real good."
– Henry Rollins

"God is near me (or rather in me), and yet I may be far from God because I may be far from my own true self."
– C. E. Rolt

"If God be for us, who can be against us?"
– Romans 8:31

"The average dog is a nicer person than the average person."
– Andy Rooney

"The future belongs to those who believe in the beauty of their dreams."
– Eleanor Roosevelt

"I think somehow we learn who we really are and then we live with that decision."
– Eleanor Roosevelt

"Today we are faced with the preeminent fact that, if civilization is to survive, we must cultivate the science of human relationships — the ability of all people, of all kinds, to live together and work together, in the same world at peace."
– Franklin Roosevelt

"My father taught me that the only way you can make good at anything is to practice, and then practice some more."
– Peter Rose

"The fundamental delusion of humanity is to suppose that I am here and you are out there."
– Yasutani Roshi

"There are only 3 colors, 10 digits, and 7 notes; it's what we do with them that's important."
– Ruth Ross

"I cannot believe that the purpose of life is to be happy. I think the purpose of life is to be useful, to be responsible, to be compassionate. It is, above all to

matter, to count, to stand for something, to have made some difference that you lived at all."
– Leo Rosten

"The truth is that the world is full of dragons, and none of us are as powerful or cool as we'd like to be. And that sucks. But when you're confronted with that fact, you can either crawl into a hole and quit, or you can get out there, take off your shoes, and Bilbo it up."
– Patrick Rothfuss

"Anger and hardness is a shield, it masks other things."
– Mickey Rourke

"The thirst after happiness is never extinguished in the heart of man."
– Jean Jacques Rousseau

"We need 'wake up economics,' where people value each other rather than the accumulation of wealth, power, and prestige."
– Anna and Christine Rowinski

"Hope is beautiful, and so are those who have it."
– Cathy Rowland

"What's most important in a friendship? Tolerance and loyalty."
– J.K. Rowling

"We do not need magic to change the world. We carry all the power we need inside ourselves already: We have the power to imagine better."
– J.K. Rowling

"It is our choices that show what we truly are, far more than our abilities."
– J.K. Rowling

"Is 'fat' really the worst thing a human being can be? Is 'fat' worse than 'vindictive,' 'jealous,' 'shallow,' 'vain,' 'boring.' or 'cruel'? Not to me."
– J.K. Rowling

"Never underestimate the power of dreams and the influence of the human spirit. We are all the same in this notion. The potential for greatness lives within each of us."
– Wilma Rudolph

"No more words. Hear only the voice within."
– Jalal ad-Din Rumi

"Out beyond ideas of wrong-doing and right-doing, there is a field. I'll meet you there"
– Jalal ad-Din Rumi

"And you? When will you begin that long journey into yourself?"
– Jalal ad-Din Rumi

"If you are irritated by every rub, how will you be polished?"
– Jalal ad-Din Rumi

"Every object, every being, is a jar full of delight. Be a connoisseur, and taste with caution. Any wine will get you high. Judge like a king, and choose the purest, not the ones adulterated with fear, or some urgency about "what's needed.""
– Jalal ad-Din Rumi

"Why are you so enchanted with this world when a gold mine lies within you? Open your eyes and come. Return to the root of the root of your own soul."
– Jalal ad-Din Rumi

"The ground's generosity takes in our compost and grows beauty! Try to be more like the ground."
– Jalal ad-Din Rumi

"Let the beauty we love be what we do."
– Jalal ad-Din Rumi

"Be like the sun for grace and mercy. Be like the night to cover others' faults. Be like running water for generosity. Be like death for rage and anger. Be like the Earth for modesty. Appear as you are. Be as you appear."
– Jalal ad-Din Rumi

"People travel to faraway places to watch, in fascination, the kind of people they ignore at home."
– Dagobert D. Runes

"Mathematics possesses not only truth, but also supreme beauty."
– Bertrand Russell

"I would never die for my beliefs because I might be wrong."
– Bertrand Russell

"The degree of one's emotions varies inversely with one's knowledge of the facts — the less you know the hotter you get."
– Bertrand Russell

"Two things are to be remembered: that a man whose opinions and theories are worth studying may be presumed to have had some intelligence, but that no man is likely to have arrived at complete and final truth on any subject whatever. When an intelligent man expresses a view which seems to us obviously absurd, we should not attempt to prove that it is somehow true, but we should try to understand how it ever came to seem true. This exercise of historical and psychological imagination at once enlarges the scope of our thinking, and helps us to realize how foolish many of our own cherished prejudices will seem to an age which has a different temper of mind."
– Bertrand Russell

"I'll match my flops with anybody's, but I wouldn't have missed them. Flops are a part of life's menu and I've never been one to miss out on any of the courses."
– Rosalind Russell

"Motivation is what gets you started. Habit is what keeps you going.
– Jim Ryun

S

"Look again at that dot. That's here. That's home. That's us. On it everyone you love, everyone you know, everyone you ever heard of, every human being who ever was, lived out their lives. The aggregate of our joy and suffering, thousands of confident religions, ideologies, and economic doctrines, every hunter and forager, every hero and coward, every creator and destroyer of civilization, every king and peasant, every young couple in love, every mother and father, hopeful child, inventor and explorer, every teacher of morals, every corrupt politician, every "superstar," every "supreme leader," every saint and sinner in the history of our species lived there – on a mote of dust suspended in a sunbeam."

– Carl Sagan

"The truth may be puzzling. It may take some work to grapple with. It may be counterintuitive. It may contradict deeply held prejudices. It may not be consonant with what we desperately want to be true. But our preferences do not determine what is true."
– Carl Sagan

"If you wish to make an apple pie truly from scratch, you must first invent the universe."
– Carl Sagan

"Anything else you're interested in is not going to happen if you can't breathe the air and drink the water. Don't sit this one out. Do something. You are by accident of fate alive at an absolutely critical moment in the history of our planet."
– Carl Sagan

"Science is a way of thinking much more than it is a body of knowledge."
– Carl Sagan

"One who meets the true reality is transformed into gold."
– Guru Granth Sahib

"I am a kind of paranoiac in reverse. I suspect people of plotting to make me happy."
– J.D. Salinger

"There is hope in dreams, imagination, and in the courage of those who wish to make those dreams a reality."
– Jonas Salk

"Our greatest responsibility is to be good ancestors."
– Jonas Salk

"The secret to happiness is to admire without desiring."
– Carl Sandburg

"What's unnatural is homophobia. Homo sapiens is the only species in all of nature that responds with hate to homosexuality."
– Alex Sanchez

"Never respond to an angry person with a fiery comeback, even if he deserves it. Don't allow his anger to become your anger."
– Bohdi Sanders

"The world is a merrier place to live if people do things more out of sincerity, not just out of formality."
– Maggy San Jose-Baas

"The wisest mind has something yet to learn."
– George Santayana

"Character is the basis of happiness and happiness the sanction of character."
– George Santayana

"Life begins on the other side of despair."
– Jean-Paul Sarte

"We must not allow other people's limited perceptions to define us."
– Virginia Satir

"The future is not some place we are going to, but one we are creating. The paths to it are not found, but made — and the activity of making them changes both the maker and the destination."
– John Schaar

"Each day comes bearing its own gifts. Untie the ribbons."
– Ruth Ann Schabacker

"Don't worry about the future. Or worry, but know that worrying is as effective as trying to solve an algebra equation by chewing bubble gum."
– Mary Schmich

"My grandfather used to say that once in your life you need a doctor, a lawyer, a preacher – but every day, three times a day, you need a farmer."
– Brenda Schoepp

"Great men are like eagles, and build their nest on some lofty solitude."
– Arthur Schopenhauer

"The task is not to see what has never been seen before, but to think what has never been thought before about what you see every day."
– Erwin Schrodinger

"Better to do something imperfectly than to do nothing flawlessly."
– Robert H. Schuller

"The only place where your dream becomes impossible is in your own thinking."
– Robert H. Schuller

"Any intelligent fool can make things bigger, more complex, and more violent. It takes a touch of genius – and a lot of courage to move in the opposite direction."
– E.F. Schumacher

"An ounce of practice is generally worth more than a ton of theory."
– E.F. Schumacher

"This life is yours. Take the power to choose what you want to do and do it well. Take the power to love what you want in life and love it honestly. Take the power to walk in the forest and be a part of nature. Take the power to control your own life. No one else can do it for you. Take the power to make your life happy."
– Susan Polis Schutz

"A man who trims himself to suit everybody will soon whittle himself away."
– Charles Schwab

"So many people walk around with a meaningless life. They seem half-asleep, even when they're busy doing things they think are important. This is because they're chasing the wrong things. The way you get meaning into your life is to devote yourself to loving others, devote yourself to your community around you, and devote yourself to creating something that gives you purpose and meaning."
– Morrie Schwartz

"The greatest discovery of any generation is that human beings can alter their lives by altering the attitudes of their minds."
– Albert Schweitzer

"Even if it's a little thing, do something for those who have need of help, something for which you get no pay but the privilege of doing it."
– Albert Schweitzer

"To the question whether I am a pessimist or an optimist, I answer that my knowledge is pessimistic, but my willing and hoping are optimistic."
– Albert Schweitzer

"At times our own light goes out and is rekindled by a spark from another person. Each of us has cause to think with deep gratitude of those who have lighted the flame within us."
– Albert Schweitzer

"While we try to teach our children all about life, our children teach us what life is all about."
– Angela Schwindt

"The height of your accomplishments will equal the depth of your convictions."
– William F. Scolavino

"Friends are the family you choose."
– Jess C. Scott

"We must break away from the widespread belief that bigger, faster, newer, and more is always better. We need to reconsider what constitutes 'wealth.'"
– Greg Seaman

"You save yourself or you remain unsaved."
– Alice Sebold

"There is no such thing as fun for the whole family."
– Jerry Seinfeld

"Any who may wish to profit himself alone from the knowledge given him, rather than serve others through the knowledge he has gained from learning, is betraying knowledge and rendering it worthless."
– Haile Selassie

"Habits of thinking need not be forever. One of the most significant findings in psychology in the last twenty years is that individuals can choose the way they think."
– Martin Seligman

"Love is a force that connects us to every strand of the universe, an unconditional state that characterizes human nature, a form of knowledge that is always there for us if only we can open ourselves to it."
– Emily Hilburn Sell

"There is healing available to us and it can come through our imagination if we honor ourselves and our situation and if we keep open to the potency of the universe, which is also the potency within us."
– Henry Seltzer

"Man is the only creature that cooks his food, and he is more subject to disease than any wild creature that dines on unrefined food."
– Dugald Semple

"He that does good to another does good also to himself."
– Lucius Annaeus Seneca

"Most powerful is he who has himself in his own power."
– Lucius Annaeus Seneca

"Love in its essence is spiritual fire."
– Lucius Annaeus Seneca

"It is not because things are difficult that we do not dare; it is because we do not dare that they are difficult."
– Lucius Annaeus Seneca

"There is no such thing as a child who hates to read; there are only children who have not found the right book."
– Frank Serafini

"Put your ear down close to your soul and listen hard."
– Anne Sexton

"Assume a virtue if you have it not."
– William Shakespeare

"There are three people in yourself: Who people think you are, Who you think you are, and who you really are."
– William Shakespeare

"All the world's a stage, and all the men and women merely players: they have their exits and their entrances; and one man in his time plays many parts."
– William Shakespeare

"We know what we are, but know not what we may be."
– William Shakespeare

"Make not your thoughts your prisons."
– William Shakespeare

"This above all: To thine own self be true, for it must follow as dost the night the day, that canst not then be false to any man."
– William Shakespeare

"Honesty is the best policy."
– William Shakespeare

"How far that little candle throws his beams! So shines a good deed in a weary world."
– William Shakespeare

"Our doubts are traitors, and make us lose the good we oft might win by fearing the attempt."
– William Shakespeare

"Reality is wrong. Dreams are for the real."
– Tupac Shakur

"Nothing in the world can bother you as much as your own mind, I tell you. In fact, others seem to be bothering you, but it is not others, it is your own mind."
– Sri Sri Ravi Shankar

"Push yourself to do more and to experience more. Harness your energy to start expanding your dreams. Yes, expand your dreams. Don't accept a life of mediocrity when you hold such infinite potential within the fortress of your mind. Dare to tap into your greatness."
– Robin S. Sharma

"Leave each person you meet a little better than when you found them."
– Robin S. Sharma

"People who say it cannot be done should not interrupt those who are doing it."
– George Bernard Shaw

"I am of the opinion that my life belongs to the community, and as long as I live it is my privilege to do for it whatever I can."
– George Bernard Shaw

"Imagination is the beginning of creation. You imagine what you desire, you will what you imagine, and at last you create what you will."
– George Bernard Shaw

"The people who get on in this world are the people who get up and look for the circumstances they want, and, if they can't find them, make them."
– George Bernard Shaw

"Some men see things as they are and say, 'Why?' I dream of things that never were, and say, 'Why not?'"
– George Bernard Shaw

"We don't stop playing because we grow old; we grow old because we stop playing."
– George Bernard Shaw

"We are made wise not by the recollection of our past, but by the responsibility for our future."
– George Bernard Shaw

"Each of us makes his own weather, determines the color of the skies in the emotional universe which he inhabits."
– Archbishop Fulton J. Sheen

"No man chooses evil because it is evil; he only mistakes it for happiness, the good he seeks."
– Mary Shelley

"When you start using senses you neglected, your reward is to see the world with completely fresh eyes."
– Barbara Sher

"Vision is perhaps our greatest strength. It has kept us alive to the power and continuity of thought through the centuries, it makes us peer into the future and lends shape to the unknown."
– Li Ka Shing

"There are cycles that recur in the heavens and cycles that recur in our lives. We're meant to learn something from every passage. We're fortunate if we discover early that superficial values never lead to happiness."
– Kate Sholly

"Success makes you less intimidated by things."
– Nate Silver

"Everything in this world is a manifestation of what you give the world. The laws of karma are in every scripture. They're in the Bible, and the Quoran, the Torah, they're in the yoga sutras. Every prophet tells you the same thing. It is really what you give the world that you get back from the world. Not that you have to trade, but give the world the positivity you want back. And you have to have faith that is what is going on. That is what is going on."
– Russell Simmons

"Do the things you want to see."
– Russell Simmons

"To touch can be to give life."
– Michelangelo di Lodovico Buonarroti Simoni

"The greatest danger for most of us is not that our aim is too high and we miss it, but that it is too low and we reach it."
– Michelangelo di Lodovico Buonarroti Simoni

"If you keep saying things are going to be bad, you have a good chance of being a prophet."
– Isaac Bashevis Singer

"We know what a person thinks not when he tells us what he thinks, but by his actions."
– Isaac Bashevis Singer

"Serve, love, give, purify, meditate, realize, be good, do good, be kind, be compassionate."
– Swami Sivananda

"Don't let the losers win. Water seeks it's own level, you have to be concerned about those that try to pull you down to their level when you're trying to rise above and do special stuff or go through change in your life. Like they say, misery loves company. You have to be aware of that."
– Nikki Sixx

"The key to getting lots of strangers to work together is not to create an endless stream of new laws or institutions, but to create a set of shared values. Laws are something you merely obey. Values are something you feel."
– Edward Slingerland

"With a little time, and a little more insight, we begin to see both ourselves and our enemies in humbler profiles. We are not really as innocent as we felt when we were first hurt. And we do not usually have a gigantic monster to forgive; we have a weak, needy, and somewhat stupid human being. When you see your enemy and yourself in the weakness and silliness of the humanity you share, you will make the miracle of forgiving a little easier."
– Lewis B. Smedes

"We often discover what will do, by finding out what will not do; and probably he who never made a mistake never made a discovery."
– Samuel Smiles

"Life is full of beauty. Notice it. Notice the bumble bee, the small child, and the smiling faces. Smell the rain, and feel the wind. Live your life to the fullest potential, and fight for your dreams."
– Ashley Smith

"In art and dream may you proceed with abandon. In life may you proceed with balance and stealth. For nothing is more precious than the life force and may the love of that force guide you as you go."
– Patti Smith

"Our thoughts, our feelings, our dreams, our ideas are physical in the universe. If we dream something, if we picture something, if we commit ourselves to it — that is a physical thrust towards realization that we can put into the universe."
– Will Smith

"When you acknowledge the obstacle you give it power by the acknowledgement of it. I'm going to walk over it. I'm going to walk around it.

I would say that my preoccupation is with the power that we all possess individually and I refuse to relinquish my power. So my preoccupation with that happening is that the belief in possibility is our power. And don't give it away for anything.

I believe very strongly that we are who we choose to be."
– Will Smith

"There is a redemptive power that making a choice has. Rather than feeling that you're an affect to all the things that are happening, make your choice. You just decide what it is going to be, who you are going to be, how you are going to do it. Just decide, and from that point, the universe is going to get out of your way. It's water. It wants to move and go around stuff."
– Will Smith

"Let him who would move the world first move himself."
– Socrates

"For as he thinketh in his heart, so is he."
– King Solomon

"Where there is no vision, the people parish."
– King Solomon

"If a person finds the negative people in his network, then he needs to mind or mend his own nature than others for his basic grounding decides only the level of acidic or toxic surrounding."
– Anuj Somany

"A man is at his best when he is simply not like the rest in all his life's test."
– Anuj Somany

"If strangers like one's quote truly, then it only means that the in-built message has enough depth, breadth, touch and connection with the life's reality."
– Anuj Somany

"Not everything is understood the way it is presented and not everyone presents the way it is understood."
– Anuj Somany

"The more you hate the more you die."
– Harry Somers

"For a chunk of my life, I avoided shy people, assuming they had nothing to say. Then one day I realized that if I quit blabbering for a minute, they'd often utter something that would blow my mind."
– Tara Somerville

"Heaven never helps the man who will not act."
– Sophocles

"A man, though wise, should never be ashamed of learning more, and must unbend his mind."
– Sophocles

"The keenest sorrow is to recognize ourselves as the sole cause of all our adversities."
– Sophocles

"Don't be afraid to ask for what you want – the worst thing that can happen is you won't get it, but if you don't ask, you likely won't get it anyway."
– Cherie Soria

"Life is a barter of choice and consequences."
– Samantha Sotto

"The only people with whom you should try to get even are those who have helped you."
– John E. Southard

"For a long time it had seemed to me that life was about to begin – real life. But there was always some obstacle in the way, something to be gotten through first, some unfinished business, time still to be served, a debt to be paid. Then life would begin. At last it dawned on me that these obstacles were my life."
– Alfred D. Souza

"When you chase a dream, you learn about yourself. You learn your capabilities and limitations, and the value of hard work and persistence."
– Nicholas Sparks

"The ultimate result of shielding men from the effects of folly is to fill the world with fools."
– Herbert Spencer

"If you don't take chances, you can't do anything in life."
– Michael Spinks

"A vegetable-based diet for children is generally more healthful than a diet containing the cholesterol, animal fat, and excessive protein found in meat and dairy products. Children and adolescents will get plenty of protein as long as they eat a variety of whole-grains, legumes, vegetables, fruits, and nuts."
– Benjamin Spock

"We have become so drug-oriented, that the idea of changing anything just through diet is kind of preposterous to a lot of people. It's almost like old medicine, like a witch doctor."
– Morgan Spurlock

"I find, by experience, that the mind and the body are more than married, for they are most intimately united; and when one suffers, the other sympathizes."
– Philip Dormer Stanhope

"Those who think they have no time for bodily exercise will sooner or later have to find time for illness."
– Edward Stanley

"Nothing strengthens the judgment and quickens the conscience like individual responsibility."
– Elizabeth Stanton

"An elementary particle is not an independently existing, unanalyzable entity. It is, in essence, a set of relationships that reach outward to other things."
– H. P. Stapp

"Community means strength that joins our strength to do the work that needs to be done. Arms to hold us when we falter. A circle of healing. A circle of friends. Someplace where we can be free."
– Starhawk

"Reach high, for stars lie hidden in your soul. Dream deep, for every dream precedes the goal."
– Pamela Vaull Starr

"Scars are just another kind of memory."
– M.L. Stedman

"Do not think that what your thoughts dwell upon is no matter. Your thoughts are making you."
– Bishop Steere

"False hope is unnecessary pain."
– Rod Steiger

"Let me listen to me, and not to them."
– Gertrude Stein

"When I face the desolate impossibility of writing five hundred pages, a sick sense of failure falls on me, and I know I can never do it. Then gradually, I write one page and then another. One day's work is all I can permit myself to contemplate."
– John Steinbeck

"Many a trip continues long after movement and time and space have ceased."
– John Steinbeck

"If you and I, everytime we pass a mirror, downgrade on how we look or complain about our looks, if we remember that a girl is watching us and that's what she is learning."
– Gloria Steinem

"There is an essence of the Divine in all living things. And each person is literally a microcosm of the universe."
– Gloria Steinem

"Our vision is more obstructed by what we think we know than by our lack of knowledge."
– Krister Stendahl

"Only the brave know how to forgive; it is the most refined and generous pitch of virtue human nature can arrive at."
– Laurence Sterne

"On this shrunken globe, men can no longer live as strangers."
– Adlai E. Stevenson

"Everyday courage has few witnesses. But yours is no less noble because no drum beats for you and no crowds shout your name."
– Robert Louis Stevenson

"Eventually everyone sits down to a banquet of consequences."
– Robert Louis Stevenson

"To know what you prefer instead of humbly saying Amen to what the world tells you you ought to prefer, is to have kept your soul alive."
– Robert Louis Stevenson

"Religion is giving people hope in a world torn about by religion."
– Jon Stewart

"You can be with one of the most beautiful women in the world and still be unhappy."
– Rod Stewart

"You are a product of your environment. So choose the environment that will best develop you toward your objective. Analyze your life in terms of its environment. Are the things around you helping you toward success — or are they holding you back?"
– W. Clement Stone

"Be careful the environment you choose for it will shape you; be careful the friends you choose for you will become like them."
– W. Clement Stone

"Aim for the moon. If you miss, you may hit a star."
– W. Clement Stone

"Words deserve respect. If you get the right ones, in the right order, you can nudge the world a little."
– Tom Stoppard

"Every exit is an entry somewhere else."
– Tom Stoppard

"All serious daring starts from within."
– Harriet Beecher Stowe

"Never give up, for that is just the place and time that the tide will turn."
– Harriet Beecher Stowe

"If you are lazy, and accept your lot, you may live in it. If you are willing to work, you can write your name anywhere you choose."
– Gene Stratton-Porter

"In life, people tend to wait for good things to come to them. And by waiting, they miss out. Usually, what you wish for doesn't fall in your lap; it falls somewhere nearby, and you have to recognize it, stand up, and put in the time and work it takes to get to it. This isn't because the universe is cruel. It's because the universe is smart. It has its own cat-string theory and knows we don't appreciate things that fall into our laps."
– Neil Strauss

"The great gift of human beings is that we have the power of empathy, we can all sense a mysterious connection to each other."
– Meryl Streep

"You have to embrace getting older. Life is precious, and when you've lost a lot of people, you realize each day is a gift."
– Meryl Streep

"A complete stranger has the capacity to alter the life of another irrevocably. This domino effect has the capacity to change the course of an entire world. That is what life is; a chain reaction of individuals colliding with others and influencing their lives without realizing it. A decision that seems miniscule to you, may be monumental to the fate of the world."
– J.D. Stroube

"We are frightened by our own solitude. Yet only in solitude can we learn to know ourselves, learn to handle our own eternity of aloneness. And love from one being to another is when two solitudes come nearer, to recognize and protect and comfort each other."
– Han Suyin

"Teaching music is not my main purpose. I want to make good citizens. If children hear fine music from the day of their birth and learn to play it, they develop sensitivity, discipline and endurance. They get a beautiful heart."
– Shinichi Suzuki

"When those you love die, the best you can do is honor their spirit for as long as you live. You make a commitment that you're going to take whatever lesson

that person or animal was trying to teach you, and you make it true in your own life... it's a positive way to keep their spirit alive in the world, by keeping it alive in yourself."
– Patrick Swayze

"It's daring to be curious about the unknown, to dream big dreams, to live outside prescribed boxes, to take risks, and above all, daring to investigate the way we live until we discover the deepest treasured purpose of why we are here."
– Luci Swindoll

"Audacity augments courage; hesitation, fear."
– Publilius Syrus

"The stupid neither forgive nor forget; the naive forgive and forget; the wise forgive but do not forget."
– Thomas Stephen Szasz

T

"Don't limit a child to your own learning, for she was born in another time."
– Rabindranath Tagore

"Let me not pray to be sheltered from dangers, but to be fearless in facing them. Let me not beg for the stilling of my pain, but for the heart to conquer it."
– Rabindranath Tagore

"Music fills the infinite between two souls."
– Rabindranath Tagore

"Partings are the beginnings of new meetings. Beginnings happen because there are endings."
– Natsuki Takaya

"Every blade of grass has its angel that bends over it and whispers, 'Grow, grow.'"
– Talmud

"We do not see things as they are. We see them as we are."
– The Talmud

"When you teach your son, you teach your son's son."
– The Talmud

"You will find, that when you have someone to love, that the face is less important than the brain, and the body is less important than the heart."
– Adrian Tan

"Water which is too pure has no fish."
– Ts'ai Ken T'an

"The human tendency toward confirmatory thinking - all of us are bias to seek information that fits what we already believe."
– Valerie Tarico

"Your life is a work of art. You are the designer of your life, the paint brush is in your hands and with every beautiful picture you paint and every opportunity you cease, will one day form into your masterpiece."
– Adam Taste

"We worry about what a child will become tomorrow, yet we forget that he is someone today."
– Stacia Tauscher

"Meditation is the tongue of the soul and the language of our spirit."
– Jeremy Taylor

"I am a part of all that I have met."
– Alfred Tennyson

"Come friends, it's not too late to seek a newer world."
– Alfred Tennyson

"Be gentle to all and stern with yourself."
– Saint Teresa of Avila

"Life is and will ever remain an equation incapable of solution, but it contains certain known factors."
– Nikola Tesla

"We crave for new sensations but soon become indifferent to them. The wonders of yesterday are today common occurrences"
–Nikola Tesla

"Let us love, since our heart is made for nothing else."
– St. Therese

"When we stop working with our hands, we cease to understand how the world really works."
– Clive Thompson

"Only when we are no longer afraid do we begin to live in every experience, painful or joyous, to live in gratitude for every moment, to live abundantly."
– Dorothy Thompson

"Thank God men cannot fly, and lay waste the sky as well as the Earth."
– Henry David Thoreau

"The language of friendship is not words but meanings."
– Henry David Thoreau

"A single gentle rain makes the grass many shades greener. So our prospects brighten on the influx of better thoughts."
– Henry David Thoreau

"It's not worth our while to let our imperfections disturb us always."
– Henry David Thoreau

"Public opinion is a weak tyrant compared with our own private opinion. What a man thinks of himself, that it is which determines, or rather indicates, his fate."
– Henry David Thoreau

"Good for the body is the work of the body, and good for the soul is the work of the soul, and good for either is the work of the other."
– Henry David Thoreau

"We are constantly invited to be who we are."
– Henry David Thoreau

"Men have become the tools of their tools."
– Henry David Thoreau

"All change is a miracle to contemplate; but it is a miracle which is taking place every instant."
– Henry David Thoreau

"If one advances confidently in the direction of his dreams, and endeavors to live the life which he has imagined, he will meet with a success unexpected in common hours."
– Henry David Thoreau

"The world is but a canvas to the imagination."
– Henry David Thoreau

"You must live in the present, launch yourself on every wave, find your eternity in each moment."
– Henry David Thoreau

"Goodness is the only investment that never fails."
– Henry David Thoreau

"We see men haying in the meadow, their heads waving like the grass they cut. In the distance, the wind seemed to bend all alike."
– Henry David Thoreau

"I know of no more encouraging fact than the unquestioned ability of man to elevate his life by conscious endeavor."
– Henry David Thoreau

"What a man thinks of himself, that is what determines, or rather, indicates his fate."
– Henry David Thoreau

"Thought is the sculptor who can create the person you want to be."
– Henry David Thoreau

"The greatest compliment that was ever paid me was when one asked what I thought, and attended to my answer."
– Henry David Thoreau

"Never look back unless you are planning to go that way."
– Henry David Thoreau

"As a single footstep will not make a path on the earth, so a single thought will not make a pathway in the mind. To make a deep physical path, we walk again and again. To make a deep mental path, we must think over and over the kind of thoughts we wish to dominate our lives."
– Henry David Thoreau

"All men want, not something to do with, but something to do, or rather something to be."
– Henry David Thoreau

"Dreams are the touchstones of our character."
– Henry David Thoreau

"You can fool too much of the people too much of the time."
– James Thurber

"All human beings should try to learn before they die what they are running from, and to, and why."
– James Thurber

"Don't ask what the world needs. Ask what makes you come alive, and go do it. Because what the world needs is people who have come alive."
– Howard Thurman

"May you overcome every darkness you face in your life with the light of your soul."
– Prem Tihan

"If more of us valued food and cheer and song above hoarded gold, it would be a merrier world."
– J. R. R. Tolkien

"If humans clear inner pollution, then they will also cease to create outer pollution."
– Eckhart Tolle

"You are not just a meaningless fragment in an alien universe, briefly suspended between life and death, allowed a few short-lived pleasures followed by pain and ultimate annihilation. Underneath your outer form, you are connected with something so vast, so immeasurable and sacred, that it cannot be spoken of."
– Eckhart Tolle

"Only people who are capable of loving strongly can also suffer great sorrow, but this same necessity of loving serves to counteract their grief and heals them."
– Count Lev Nikolayevich "Leo" Tolstoy

"It has been said that art is a tryst, for in the joy of it maker and beholder meet."
– Kojiro Tomita

"If you read a lot of books you are considered well read. But if you watch a lot of TV, you're not considered well viewed."
– Lily Tomlin

"I always wanted to be somebody, but I should have been more specific."
– Lily Tomlin

"All healing is first a healing of the heart."
– Carl Townsend

"The supreme accomplishment is to blur the line between work and play."
– Arnold J. Toynbee

"No one lives long enough to learn everything they need to learn starting from scratch. To be successful, we absolutely, positively have to find people who have already paid the price to learn the things that we need to learn to achieve our goals."
– Brian Tracy

"If you wish to achieve worthwhile things in your personal and career life, you must become a worthwhile person in your own self-development."
– Brian Tracy

"Every great dream begins with a dreamer. Always remember, you have within you the strength, the patience, and the passion to reach for the stars to change the world."
– Harriet Tubman

"Books are the carriers of civilization. Without books, history is silent, literature dumb, science crippled, thought and speculation at a standstill."
– Barbara Tuchman

"If we wait for the moment when everything, absolutely everything is ready, we shall never begin."
– Ivan Turgenev

"Dreams are renewable. No matter what our age or condition, there are still untapped possibilities within us and new beauty waiting to be born."
– Dale E. Turner

"The real power behind whatever success I have now was something I found within myself — something that's in all of us, I think, a little piece of God just waiting to be discovered."
– Tina Turner

"If ya keep on doing what you've always done, you'll keep on getting what you've always got."
– Momma Turtle

"I've had a lot of worries in my life, most of which never happened."
– Mark Twain

"What gets us into trouble is not what we don't know. It's what we know for sure that just ain't so."
– Mark Twain

"Twenty years from now you will be more disappointed by the things you didn't do than by the ones you did do. So throw off the bowlines. Sail away from the safe harbor. Catch the trade winds in your sails. Explore. Dream. Discover."
– Mark Twain

"When I was a boy of fourteen, my father was so ignorant I could hardly stand to have the old man around. But when I got to be twenty-one, I was astonished at how much he had learned in seven years."
– Mark Twain

"Kindness is the language which the deaf can hear and the blind can see."
– Mark Twain

"I have known a great many troubles, but most of them never happened."
– Mark Twain

"The secret of getting ahead is getting started. The secret of getting started is breaking your complex overwhelming tasks into small manageable tasks, and then starting on the first one."
– Mark Twain

"A man cannot be comfortable without his own approval."
– Mark Twain

"We are always too busy for our children; we never give them the time or interest they deserve. We lavish gifts upon them; but the most precious gift — our personal association, which means so much to them — we give grudgingly."
– Mark Twain

"Life does not consist mainly, or even largely, of facts and happenings. It consists mainly of the storm of thought that is forever flowing through one's head."
– Mark Twain

"Forgiveness is the fragrance the violet sheds on the heel that has crushed it."
– Mark Twain

"I have been through some terrible things in my life, some of which actually happened."
– Mark Twain

"Every moment of every day we can bring this consciousness to our choices about our money, our time, and our talents to take a stand for what we believe in."
– Lynne Twist

"When you let go of trying to get more of what you don't really need, it frees up oceans of energy to make a difference with what you have."
– Lynne Twist

"I'm beginning to think that maybe it's not just how much you love someone. Maybe what matters is who you are when you're with them."
– Anne Tyler

"For me, I am driven by two main philosophies: know more today about the world than I knew yesterday and lessen the suffering of others. You'd be surprised how far that gets you."
– Neil deGrasse Tyson

"Do you have patience to wait till your mud settles and the water is clear? Can you remain unmoving till the right action arises by itself?"
– Lao Tzu

"He who knows others is wise; he who knows himself is enlightened."
– Lao Tzu

"If you want to awaken all of humanity, then awaken all of yourself. If you want to eliminate the suffering in the world then eliminate all that is dark and negative in yourself. Truly, the greatest gift you have to give is that of your own self-transformation."
– Lao Tzu

"When I let go of what I am, I become what I might be."
— Lao Tzu

"To lead people, walk behind them."
— Lao Tzu

"To see things in the seed, that is genius."
— Lao Tzu

"If you do not change direction, you may end up where you are headed."
— Lao Tzu

U

"What we love determines what we seek. What we seek determines what we think and do. What we think and do determines who we are — and who we will become."
– Dieter F. Uchtdorf

"Hurt not others with that which pains yourself."
– Udanavarga 5:18

"I learned from them that inspiration does not come like a bolt, nor is it kinetic, energetic striving, but it comes into us slowly and quietly and all the time, though we must regularly and every day give it a little chance to start flowing, prime it with a little solitude and idleness."
– Brenda Ueland

"If you have the guts to be yourself, other people'll pay your price."
– John Updike

V

"How do you go from where you are to where you want to be? I think you have to have an enthusiasm for life. You have to have a dream, a goal, and you have to be willing to work for it."
– Jim Valvano

"The art of teaching is the art of assisting discovery."
– Mark Van Doren

"The depth of darkness to which you can descend and still live is an exact measure of the height to which you can aspire to reach."
– Laurens Van du Post

"Be glad of life because it gives you the chance to love and to work and to play and to look up at the stars."
– Henry Van Dyke

"You are the books you read, the films you watch, the music you listen to, the people you meet, the dreams you have, the conversations you engage in. You are what you take from these. You are the sound of the ocean, the breath of fresh air, the brightest light and the darkest corner.
You are a collective of every experience you have had in your life. You are every single second of every single day. So drown yourself in a sea of knowledge and existence. Let the words run through your veins and let the colors fill your mind until there is nothing left to do but explode. There are no wrong answers. Inspiration is everything. Sit back, relax, and take it all in.
Now, go out and create something."
– Jac Vanek

"It takes a variety of people to challenge us, encourage us, promote us, and most of all, help us to achieve a broader dimension of ourselves."
– Glenn Van Ekeren

"Let's not forget that the little emotions are the great captains of our lives and we obey them without realizing it."
– Vincent Van Gogh

"How can I be useful, of what service can I be? There is something inside me, what can it be?"
– Vincent Van Gogh

"I am always doing what I cannot do yet, in order to learn how to do it."
– Vincent van Gogh

"How right it is to love flowers and the greenery of pines and ivy and hawthorn hedges; they have been with us from the very beginning."
– Vincent van Gogh

"People are longing to rediscover true community. We have had enough of loneliness, independence, and competition."
– Jean Vanier

"Be not angry that you cannot make others as you wish them to be, since you cannot make yourself as you wish to be."
– Thomas Van Kempen

"In unchaining others, we unchain ourselves."
– Chris Victor

"What we do flows from who we are."
– Paul Vitale

"You want to become aware of your thoughts, you want to choose your thoughts carefully and you want to have fun with this, because you are the masterpiece of your own life. You are the Michelangleo of your own life. The David that you are sculpting is you. You do it with your thoughts."
– Joe Vitale

"They alone live, who live for others."
– Swami Vivekananda

"Anything that makes weak – physically, intellectually, and spiritually – reject it as poison."
– Swami Vivekananda

"A thought is an act of creation. It is what we are here for, to create, to bring into being ourself by means of thinking."
– Marcel Vogel

"It is difficult to free fools from the chains they revere."
– Voltaire

"The art of medicine consists of amusing the patient while nature cures the disease."
– Voltaire

"I am more and more convinced that our happiness or our unhappiness depends far more on the way we meet the events of life than on the nature of those events themselves."
– Wilhelm von Humboldt

"We are flawed creatures, all of us. Some of us think that means we should fix our flaws. But get rid of my flaws and there would be no one left."
– Sarah Vowell

"Life isn't about having, it's about being. You could surround yourself with all that money can buy, and you'd still be as miserable as a human can be. I know people with perfect bodies who don't have half the happiness I've found. On my journeys I've seen more joy in the slums of Mumbai and the orphanages of Africa than in wealthy gated communities and on sprawling estates worth millions. Why is that? You'll find contentment when your talents and passion are completely engaged, in

full force. Recognize instant self-gratification for what it is. Resist the temptation to grab for material objects like the perfect house, the coolest clothes or the hottest car. The if I just had X, I would be happy syndrome is a mass delusion. When you look for happiness in mere objects, they are never enough. Look around. Look within."
– Nick Vujicic

"If I wanted to become a tramp, I would seek information and advice from the most successful tramp I could find. If I wanted to become a failure, I would seek advice from people who never succeeded. If I wanted to succeed in all things, I would look around me for those who are succeeding, and do as they have done."
– Joseph Marshall Wade

"I am convinced that there are universal currents of Divine thought vibrating the ether everywhere and that any who can feel these vibrations is inspired."
– Richard Wagner

"It's not what you are that holds you back, it's what you think you are not."
– Denis Waitley

"Our limitations and success will be based, most often, on our own expectations for ourselves. What the mind dwells upon, the body acts upon."
– Denis Waitely

"Time is an equal opportunity employer. Each human being has exactly the same number of hours and minutes every day. Rich people can't buy more hours. Scientists can't invent new minutes. And you can't save time to spend it on another day. Even so, time is amazingly fair and forgiving. No matter how much time you've wasted in the past, you still have an entire tomorrow."
– Denis Waitely

"By thinking and acting affirmatively in this minute, you will influence the hour, the day, and the time, your entire life."
– Denis Waitley

"Everything takes time. Bees have to move very fast to stay still."
– David Foster Wallace

"Why are you trying so hard to fit in when you were born to stand out?"
– Ian Wallace

"Every man dies, but not every man truly lives."
– William Wallace

"If you want the best the world has to offer, offer the world your best."
– Neale Donald Walsch

"Among the problems with shame was that it in fact did not make you shorter or quieter or less visible. You just felt like you were."
– J.R. Ward

"The adventure of life is to learn. The purpose of life is to grow. The nature of life is to change. The challenge of life is to overcome. The essence of life is to care. The opportunity of like is to serve. The secret of life is to dare. The spice of life is to befriend. The beauty of life is to give."
– William Arthur Ward

"We can choose to throw stones, to stumble on them, to climb over them, or to build with them."
– William Arthur Ward

"Three keys to more abundant living: caring about others, daring for others, sharing with others."
– William A. Ward

"An artist is somebody who produces things that people don't need to have."
– Any Warhol

"There is no moment of delight in any pilgrimage like the beginning of it."
– Charles Dudley Warner

"We are products of our past, but we don't have to be prisoners of it."
– Rick Warren

"There are two ways of exerting one's strength: one is pushing down, the other is pulling up."
– Booker T. Washington

"Tell not your dreams, but to your intimate friend."
– George Washington

"Don't live down to expectations. Go out there and do something remarkable."
– Wendy Wasserstein

"To invent your own life's meaning is not easy, but it's still allowed, and I think you'll be happier for the trouble."
– Bill Watterson

"Do not sit down and try to attract the thing you want to you; but begin to move toward the thing you want, and you will find it coming to meet you. Action and reaction are equal; and the person who steadily and purposefully moves forward with one thing in view, becomes a center toward which the thing he seeks is drawn with irresistible power."
– Wallace D. Wattles

"Meditation is the discovery that the point of life is always arrived at in the immediate moment."
– Alan Watts

"No matter how ugly the world gets or how stupid it shows me it is, I always have faith."
– Gerard Way

"Our Western institutional religious tradition has essentially repressed and distorted the sexual instinct and thereby created a variety of personal and social pathologies. In so doing it has also effectively removed sexuality from its spiritual foundation."
– Gunther Weil

"Imagination and fiction make up more than three quarters of our real life."
– Simone Weil

"Words can never fully say what we want them to say, for they fumble, stammer, and break the best porcelain. The best one can hope for is to find along the way someone to share the path, content to walk in silence, for the heart communes best when it does not try to speak."
– Margaret Weis

"Movement is a medicine for creating change in a person's physical, emotional, and mental states."
– Carol Welch

"I am a writer who came from a sheltered life. A sheltered life can be a daring life as well. For all serious daring starts from within."
– Eudora Welty

"Do all the good you can. By all the means you can. In all the ways you can. In all the places you can. At all the times you can. To all the people you can. As long as ever you can."
– John Wesley

"I never said it would be easy, I only said it would be worth it."
– Mae West

"There are two ways of spreading light; to be the candle or the mirror that reflects it."
– Edith Wharton

"If only we'd stop trying to be happy we'd have a pretty good time."
– Edith Wharton

"The scientific search for the basic building blocks of life has revealed a startling fact: there are none. The deeper that physicists peer into the nature of reality, the only thing they find is relationships. Even sub-atomic particles do not exist alone. One physicist described neutrons, electrons, etc. as 'a set of relationships that reach outward to other things.' Although physicists still name them as separate, these particles aren't ever visible until they're in relationship with other particles. Everything in the Universe is composed of these 'bundles of potentiality' that only manifest their potential in relationship."
– Margaret J. Wheatley

"The whole problem is to establish communication with one's self."
– E. B. White

"Children are the living messages we send to a time we will not see."
– John W. Whitehead

"Re-examine all you have been told at school or church or in any book, dismiss whatever insults your own soul, and your very flesh shall be a great poem."
– Walt Whitman

"Pointing to another world will never stop vice among us; shedding light over this world can alone help us."
– Walt Whitman

"Of all sad words of mouth or pen, the saddest are these: it might have been."
– John Greenleaf Whittier

"I had gone through life thinking I was better than everyone else and at the same time, being afraid of everyone. I was afraid to be me."
– Dennis Wholey

"It's how we spend our time here and now, that really matters. If you are fed up with the way you have come to interact with time, change it."
– Marcia Wieder

"The only people who really think they have seen something new are those whose experience is limited or whose vision can't penetrate beneath the surface of things. Because something is recent, they think it is new; they mistake now the for originality."
– Warren W. Wiersbe

"Every thought has the power to bring into being the visible from the invisible. It is absolutely necessary for us all to understand that everything we think, do, or say comes back to us. Every thought, word, or action – without exception – manifests itself as an actual reality."
– Ann Wigmore

"The food you eat can either be the safest and most powerful form of medicine, or the slowest form of poison."
– Ann Wigmore

"Let it never be said that I was silent when they needed me."
– William Wilberforce

"There is no chance, no destiny, no fate, that can hinder or control the firm resolve of a determined soul."
– Ella Wheeler Wilcox

"With every deed you are sowing a seed, though the harvest you may not see."
– Ella Wheeler Wilcox

"Life is a pilgrimage. The wise man does not rest by the roadside inns. He marches direct to the illimitable domain of eternal bliss, his ultimate destination."
– Oscar Wilde

"Most people are other people. Their thoughts are someone else's opinions, their lives a mimicry, their passions a quotation."
– Oscar Wilde

"Patriotism is the virtue of the vicious."
– Oscar Wilde

"Life has been your art. You have set yourself to music. Your days are your sonnets."
– Oscar Wilde

"But we never get back our youth… The pulse of joy that beats in us at twenty becomes sluggish. Our limbs fail, our senses rot. We degenerate into hideous puppets, haunted by the memory of the passions of which we were too much afraid, and the exquisite temptations that we had not the courage to yield to."
– Oscar Wilde

"What seems to us as bitter trials are often blessings in disguise."
– Oscar Wilde

"Some cause happiness wherever they go, others whenever they go."
– Oscar Wilde

"Be yourself. Everyone else is already taken."
– Oscar Wilde

"You don't love someone for their looks, or their clothes, or for their fancy car, but because they sing a song only you can hear."
– Oscar Wilde

"Any place that we love becomes our world."
– Oscar Wilde

"Excuses are the nails used to build a house of failure."
– Don Wilder

"We can only be said to be alive in those moments when our hearts are conscious of our treasures."
– Thornton Wilder

"Education is the mother of leadership."
– Wendell Willkie

"Miracles start to happen when you give as much energy to your dreams as you do to your fears."
– Richard Wilkins

"The world is wide, and I will not waste my life in friction when it could be turned into momentum."
– Frances E. Willard

"Mankind is not the only abimal that laughs, cries, thinks, feels, and loves. The sooner we acknowledge that animals are emotional beings, the sooner we will cease

destroying animals and embrace them as our brothers and sisters."
– Anthony Douglas Williams

"Good words bring good feelings to the heart. Speak with kindness, always."
– Rod Williams

"Procrastination is the passive assassin of opportunity."
– Roy Williams

"Everyday, our species participates in the mass genocide of other species without care or concern or even questioning whether the violence that we ingest and condone plays any role in our apathetic support of the war machine we have become. How is it that we as human beings can represent both the highest and most developed and lowest and least concerned forms of intelligence of any living species? Are we simply glued to age-old barbaric traditions that cloud our senses and render us inhumane in our dependence on comfort foods and practices? Is our dependence on foreign oil the only thing we need to curb? What about not so foreign species?"
– Saul Williams

"Ya gotta be ready for the fastball."
– Ted Williams

"I have inherited a belief in community, the promise that a gathering of the spirit can both create and change culture. In the desert, change is nurtured even in stone by wind, by water, through time."
– Terry Tempest Williams

"Make voyages. Attempt them. There's nothing else."
– Tennessee Williams

"The best form of revenge is success."
– Vanessa Williams

"You have to believe in yourself when no one else does. That's what makes you a winner."
– Venus Williams

"Personal transformation can and does have global affects. As we go, so goes the world, for the world is us. The revolution that will save the world is ultimately a personal one."
– Marianne Williamson

"As we are liberated from our own fear, our presence automatically liberates others."
– Marianne Williamson

"We ask ourselves, who am I to be brilliant, gorgeous, handsome, talented and fabulous? Actually, who are you not to be?"
– Marianne Williamson

"As we let our light shine, we unconsciously give other people permission to do the same."
– Marianne Williamson

"Our deepest fear is not that we are inadequate. Our deepest fear is that we are powerful beyond measure. It is our light not our darkness that most frightens us. We ask ourselves, who am I to be brilliant, gorgeous, talented and fabulous? Actually, who are you not to be?

You are a child of God. Your playing small does not serve the world. There's nothing enlightened about shrinking so that other people won't feel insecure around you.

We were born to make manifest the glory of God that is within us. It's not just in some of us; it's in everyone. And as we let our own light shine, we unconsciously give other people permission to do the same. As we are liberated from our own fear, our presence automatically liberates others."
– Marianne Williamson

"Thought is cause: experience is effect. If you don't like the effects in your life, you have to change the nature of your thinking."
– Marianne Williamson

"You are responsible for the world that you live in. It is not the government's responsibility. It is not your school's or your social club's or your church's or your neighbor's or your fellow citizen's. It is yours, utterly and singularly yours."
– August Wilson

"To the world you may be one person but to one person you may be the world."
– Bill Wilson

"You are precisely as big as what you love and precisely as small as what you allow to annoy you."
– Robert Anton Wilson

"You are not here merely to make a living. You are here in order to enable the world to live more amply, with greater vision, with a finer spirit of hope and achievement. You are here to enrich the world, and you impoverish yourself if you forget the errand."
– Woodrow Wilson

"If you want to make enemies, try to change something."
– Woodrow T. Wilson

"Energy is the essence of life. Every day you decide how you're going to use it by knowing what you want and what it takes to reach that goal, and by maintaining focus."
– Oprah Winfrey

"Real integrity is doing the right thing, knowing that nobody's going to know whether you did it or not."
– Oprah Winfrey

"I've come to believe that each of us has a personal calling that's as unique as a fingerprint — and that the best way to succeed is to discover what you love and then find a way to offer it to others in the form of service, working hard, and also allowing the energy of the universe to lead you."
– Oprah Winfrey

"Assumptions are the termites of relationships."
– Henry Franklin Winkler

"Don't be content in your life just to do no wrong. Be prepared every day to try and do some good."
– Nicolas Winton

"Just because a man lacks the use of his eyes doesn't mean he lacks vision."
– Stevie Wonder

"Defeat is not the worst of failures. Not to have tried is the true failure."
– George E. Woodberry

"Do not let what you cannot do interfere with what you can do."
– John Wooden

"You can stand tall without standing on someone. You can be a victor without having victims."
– Harriet Woods

"Yet it is in our idleness, in our dreams, that the submerged truth sometimes comes to the top."
– Virginia Woolf

"Not choice, but habit rules the unreflecting herd."
– William Wordsworth

"Our birth is but a sleep and a forgetting: the soul that rises with us, our life's star, hath had elsewhere its setting, and cometh from afar. Not in entire forgetfulness and not in utter nakedness, but trailing clouds of glory do we come, from God, who is our home."
– William Wordsworth

"His high endeavors are an inward light, that makes the path before him always bright."
– William Wordsworth

"The real tragedy of life is not in being limited to one talent, but in the failure to use that one talent."
– Edgar W. Work

"The heart is the chief feature of a functioning mind."
– Frank Lloyd Wright

"Less is only more where more is no good."
– Frank Lloyd Wright

"I believe in God, only I spell it Nature."
– Frank Lloyd Wright

"Education is the passport to the future, for tomorrow belongs to those who prepare for it today."
– Malcolm X

"An English writer telephoned me from London, asking questions. One was, 'What's your alma mater?' I told him, 'Books.'"
– Malcolm X

Y

"Sometimes you have to take the leap, and build your wings on the way down."
– Kobi Yamada

"We're here, and then we're gone, and it's not about the time we're here, but what we do with the time."
– Rick Yancey

"In dreams begins responsibility."
– William Butler Yeats

"Education is not the filling of a pail, but the lighting of a fire."
– William Butler Yeats

"The mind is not a vessel to be filled, but a fire to be kindled."
– William Butler Yeats

"Education is not the filling of a pail, but the lighting of a fire."
– William Butler Yeats

"Making others happy, through kindness of speech and sincerity of right advice, is a sign of true greatness. To hurt another soul by sarcastic words, looks, or suggestions, is despicable."
– Paramahansa Yogananda

"Truths are universally and not individually rooted; a truth cannot be created, but only perceived."
– Paramahansa Yogananda

"Always remember that you belong to no one, and no one belongs to you. Reflect that some day you will suddenly have to leave everything in this world – so make the acquaintanceship of God now."
– Paramhansa Yogananda

"Again and again I will suffer; again and again I will get back on my feet. I will not be defeated. I won't let my spirit be destroyed."
– Banana Yoshimoto

"Procrastination is the thief of time."
– Edward Young

"Often people attempt to live their lives backwards: they try to have more things, or more money, in order to do more of what they want so they will be happier. The way it actually works is the reverse. You must first be

who you really are, then do what you need to do, in order to have what you want."
– Margaret Young

"A man doesn't need to be flawless to be a perfect father, but the commitment to his family is a precious responsibility."
– Paul Young

"The truth is that there is nothing noble in being superior to somebody else. The only real nobility is in being superior to your former self."
– Whitney Young

"My greatest challenge has been to change the mindset of people. Mindsets play strange tricks on us. We see things the way our minds have instructed our eyes to see."
– Muhammad Yunus

Z

"Conversation is a meeting of minds with different memories and habits. When minds meet, they don't just exchange facts: they transform them, reshape them, draw different implications from them, engage in new trains of thought. Conversation doesn't just reshuffle the cards: it creates new cards."
– Theodore Zeldin

"If you cannot find the truth right where you are, where else do you expect to find it?"
– Dogen Zenji

"Our thinking about non-human animals is very confused, and people who have chosen to live a cruelty-free plant-based lifestyle are baffled as to why other people have not made the connection. Many of us live

with companion animals such as dogs, cats, and rabbits. We share our homes with them, consider them members of the family and we grieve when they die. Yet we kill and eat other animals who, if you really think about it, are no different from the ones we love."
– Banjamin Zephaniah

"Always forgive, but never forget, else you will be a prisoner of your own hatred, and doomed to repeat your mistakes forever."
– Wil Zeus

"I dreamed I was a butterfly, flitting around in the sky; then I awoke. Now I wonder: Am I a man who dreamt of being a butterfly, or am I a butterfly dreaming that I am a man?"
– Zhuangzi

"A lot of people have gone further than they thought they could because someone else thought they could"
– Zig Ziglar

"May you see sunshine where others see shadows, and opportunities where others see obstacles."
– Zig Ziglar

"A lot of people quit looking for work as soon as they find a job."
– Zig Ziglar

"Put all excuses aside and remember this: you are capable."
– Zig Ziglar

"You are the only person on earth who can use your ability."
– Zig Ziglar

"People often say that motivation doesn't last. Well, neither does bathing — that's why we recommend it daily."
– Zig Ziglar

"Don't be distracted by criticism. Remember the only taste of success some people have is when they take a bite out of you."
– Zig Ziglar

"Who would bring light must endure burning."
– David Zindell

"War itself is enemy to the human race."
– Howard Zinn

"When we make a conscious decision to create – to make a painting for instance – we are opening the door to the pure source energy flowing through us and asking that we become able to interpret it in a way that we and others may understand it. Fasting is the greatest way that I know of to achieve ultimate clarity in this process – to tap directly into the source in order to bring back information via visual language that will inspire growth and awareness in others. Art is free to all without rules – how can anyone pass that up? Art is our responsibility – it is the essential catalyst for universal shift."
– Zito

"By choosing your thoughts, and by selecting which emotional currents you will release and which you will reinforce, you determine the quality of your light. You determine the effects that you will have upon others, and the nature of the experience of your life."
– Gary Zukav

"Emotions reflect intentions. Therefore, awareness of emotions leads to awareness of intentions."
– Gary Zukav

"In the world to come they will not ask me, 'Why were you not Moses?' They will ask me, 'Why were you not Zusya?'"
– Reb Zusya

ABOUT THE AUTHOR

"The act of writing is an act of optimism. You would not take the trouble to do it if you felt it didn't matter."
– Edward Albee

John McCabe has written a variety of books relating to health, food, thought, and environmental issues.

McCabe's first book was *Surgery Electives: What to Know Before the Doctor Operates*. It was an exposé of the financial ties of the medical school, hospital, pharmaceutical, and health insurance industries whose unethical business practices result in the deaths of tens of thousands of people in the U.S. every year. The book was endorsed by some congresspersons and by all of the patients' rights groups in North America.

McCabe also wrote a similar book specific for those considering cosmetic surgery. *Plastic Surgery Hopscotch* was published in 1995 and detailed many of the risks involved with the various surgeries.

Realizing that medical care in Western culture is largely the end result of horrible dietary choices, McCabe turned to writing about how a plant-based diet can prevent and reverse a wide variety of diseases while also protecting the environment.

Becoming an advocate for plant-based nutrition free of disease-inducing animal protein, synthetic chemicals, heat-generated toxins, and rancid and fried oils, McCabe wrote books including *Sunfood Diet Infusion*, *Sunfood Traveler*, *Vegan Myth Vegan Truth*, *Hollywood Crew Health Revival Plan*, and *Raw Vegan Easy Healthy Recipes*. He also helped other authors write their books on similar topics.

As a way to expose the dire situation of the damaged environment, including from ocean acidification, mountaintop removal, fracking, tar sands mining, clearcutting, nuclear energy, animal agriculture, monocropping, and the spread of industrial pollutants, and to help educate people on the need for a more sustainable society, including the need to shut down the animal farming cartels and stop the GMO companies, McCabe wrote a little book titled *Extinction: The Death of Waterlife on Planet Earth*. In it, McCabe continues his advocacy for a plant-based diet free.

In tune with healthy living, McCabe wrote a book titled *Igniting Your Life*. The book combines philosophical and motivational quotations from throughout history with commentary relating to leading a healthy, goal-oriented, happy life.

McCabe is the author of *Marijuana & Hemp: History, Uses, Laws, and Controversy*, which details the uses of the world's most useful industrial plant, which can be used for everything from construction materials, to fabric, food, and fuel. The book explains how corrupt politicians have worked with corporate leaders to outlaw industrial hemp farming in the U.S. and many other countries.

Have you found this book helpful?

Let others know about it.
Post about it on Facebook.
Tweet about it on Twitter.
Snap a photo of the cover and text or email it to a friend.
Write a customer review on the book's Amazon.com page.
Gift a copy to a friend, relative, neighbor, or associate.
Give a copy to a graduate.
Drop a copy at a homeless shelter.
Leave a copy on someone's doorstep.

Uplift.
Encourage.
Compliment.
Bring good tidings.
Build confidence.

Make a game plan, and play it daily.

www.ingramcontent.com/pod-product-compliance
Lightning Source LLC
Chambersburg PA
CBHW070546050426
42450CB00011B/2743